AN AMERICAN RAILROAD DREAM

AN AMERICAN RAILROAD DREAM

My Life as a Railroad Engineer

SUSIE GAGLIA

with a foreword by Patrick C. Morrison, director
Railroad Museum of Pennsylvania

Haley's
Athol, Massachusetts

Haley's
488 South Main Street
Athol, MA 01331
haley.antique@verizon.net
800.215.8805

Photos and mementos from the author's collection.
Copy edited by Debra Ellis.
Special thanks to Chris Coyle.

Library of Congress Control Number: pending

Cataloguing in Publishing data: pending
    ISBN 978-0-9967730-6-5 (trade paperback)
    ISBN 978-0-9967730-9-6 (hardcover)

to my sister, Bonnie,
who grew up by my side and
encouraged and supported me and
my dream to the end

Contents

Illustrations

Susie, a Trailblazer

a foreword by Patrick C. Morrison
director, Railroad Museum of Pennsylvania

When I first met Susie during her visit to our museum in Strasburg, Pennsylvania, on April 22, 2017, I was captivated by Susie's spirit, her great enthusiasm for trains, and her many treasured memories of her work on the railroad. I have always thought that if I could have *ten* great years doing something that I love professionally, then I could die happy. Well, Susie had *fifteen* years doing just that—something that she loved—*and still does.*

During her visit, I had an opportunity to walk with Susie around the Railroad Museum of Pennsylvania's spacious Rolling Stock Hall. During her visit, she climbed aboard several of the locomotives that she once operated, including the GG1 4935, the E44 4465, and the GP30 2233. With the help of Curator Allan Martin, we also climbed inside the Amtrak AEM7 915, which is stored outdoors. The 915 is a favorite of Susie's. It's one of my favorites, too. All the while, you could see her eyes light up as she sat in the engineer's seat, no doubt remembering what it was like to power a heavy freight train or a speedy passenger train.

There were some things I wanted to ask Susie, but I was afraid to do so. While I had only just met her despite the two of us having corresponded back and forth for a few weeks prior to her visit, I knew there was much more to her story than what she could share with me that day. While she did not speak of the struggle that she must have undoubtedly endured in a male-dominated profession, I could tell that the job was not always as glorious and glamorous as it is portrayed in children's storybooks and in the popular consciousness, especially for women.

That is why I feel honored to have met Susie, a trailblazer and a hero in my view. And when I look at my mother's generation and of those who followed, especially my wife and my young daughter, I am very grateful to Susie and others for helping blaze that trail to diversify our workforce and opportunities available to women. When I look at my daughter, I think, *You can follow your dream, just as Susie has done*.

In 1978, when Susie began her career as a locomotive engineer, women were still very much outsiders within the operating crafts in the railroad industry. More than a century earlier, women like Susie were more likely to take on clerical or domestic roles in the railroad industry. By the 1850s, women began to be hired as telegraphers, secretaries, operators, and agents, although among less frequented stations. While American history carries countless examples of women entering the railroad workforce as attendants, shop workers, and car cleaners—even occasionally as engineers and firemen—opportunities beyond the more traditional roles for women always appear few and far between. Even where progress seemed evident, efforts restricted the numbers of hours women worked and the kinds of positions they held.

During World Wars I and II, to replace the draft-diminished male workforce, women were employed in large numbers in virtually every area of the industry. However, when soldiers returned home, women often found themselves either laid off or retaining less-coveted and traditionally female clerical and domestic duties. Their extraordinary efforts during those years proved that women could not only do the jobs that men did, they did them—and quite well. They could also hold down families and take care of their homes at the same time. By the 1960s, the situation began to change again, if very gradually. In the early twenty-first century, although much has improved, Class I railroads—and other industries—can do much more to level the playing field. Opportunities continue to arise, and women continue to prove themselves more than equal to the task.

The preceding simply provides historical context for the meeting that took place on April 22, 2017. It was just an ordinary day for some, but not for me. For me, it was not ordinary. I was just a few weeks away from starting a new job as director of the Railroad Museum of Pennsylvania, and I experienced the time with Susie as distinctly special. When I meet people who worked for a railroad, I often think about the fact that challenges I will face in my new job are nothing when compared to what railroaders like Susie must have experienced on a regular basis: being on call 24/7 and enduring long hours on the road away from home and family, unplanned equipment and maintenance headaches, and dangers on the right-of-way—*just to name a few*.

When I see how thrilled and overjoyed Susie was to be back in the engineer's seats of some of the locomotives she once operated, I can imagine much more of her story. As I begin a new chapter in my own career, I long to learn more from each important and exciting chapter in Susie's time as a locomotive engineer.

And what an amazing journey it must have been! Like you, I am glad I cracked open this book to read Susie's reminiscences about her time "on the road" as an engineer for Amtrak and Conrail.

All aboard!

My Story and My Experiences

an introduction by Susie Gaglia

Through the years, I met new people, and we shared interesting conversations. It amazed them all when I told them I had been a railroad engineer—that, yes, I actually did run trains.

I had their full attention, and they wanted to hear more. I began to hear, "You should write a book." I smiled whenever it happened, and that's how it all started.

This book tells my story about my experiences and my life as a railroad locomotive engineer for ConRail/Amtrak from 1978 to 1993.

The Distant Train Whistle

It is 12:01 in the morning, July 4, 1953. A baby girl is born, a real firecracker: me.

My mom had no idea what kind of future her spunky little bundle of joy would create.

We lived in the small town of Orchard Park, New York, south of Buffalo. The busy local railroad seemed to run trains all day and night. We heard them rumbling down the rails blowing their whistles for road crossings. It became second nature for us who lived there. If we didn't hear them, we thought something was wrong.

So, at the very beginning stages of my life I learned to recognize the sound of a distant train whistle. My mom later told stories about how I kicked my feet, clapped my hands, and smiled when trains ran by blowing their whistles. Mom said with a smile that my first words were "MaMa choo-choo."

Through the years, I heard trains and their lonesome whistles in the distance, and I learned to love that sound. It felt like a faraway voice calling to me.

*Susie, left, and
her sister Bonnie in 1955*

In 1958, my Dad put my Cousin Doug's Lionel train set around the Christmas tree when I was five. We were all so excited. After all, that magical, warm, and happy time of year brought the whole family together. I lay on my stomach and watched the train go around and around, colored lights from the tree reflecting on its every move. Sometimes the train stopped in front of me, and I pointed my tiny finger in the cab window of the locomotive and said, "I'm gonna be an engineer and blow the whistle." Everyone laughed.

The years rolled on, and I turned seven. My dad wanted to build a small train table in the basement. I was all for that and wanted to help. It was HO scale, my very own first train set, but I think my dad really thought it belonged to him because he was in charge, he was the boss, he was the engineer (I think all dads know what I mean). It took awhile, but after hammering thousands of tiny nails into a piece of plywood, it was time to connect the transformer. That was Dad's job. My job was to place the train on the track.

And then the moment of long anticipated joy. Dad pushed the transformer lever forward and the light on the locomotive came on, but the engine needed that first little push to get started. And wow! That was awesome! Our very own railroad! I wore my grandfather's original conductor's hat. I loved my grandfather, and I loved that black hat with a gold band. He worked for the

Susie's sister Bonnie, left, Susie, and their Cousin Doug with a Lionel train set in 1958

Delaware, Lackawanna, and Western Railroad. My dad said, "You got railroad blood in you, Kid." I smiled and felt proud.

I didn't know then that the little home railroad built by my father and me would remain with me the rest of my life.

Waiting for the Train

In September, 1963, when I was ten, my friend PJ, the boy who lived across the street, located the best nearby railroad crossing we could ride our bikes to and sit and wait for the train.

Eventually we got the timing of train arrivals close to within the hour, and we always showed up on time at the crossing. On our days off and sometimes after school, we rode our bikes to the railroad crossing to wait for the train. As we waited, we threw ballast rocks across the tracks and placed our pennies on the track to be flattened by the weight of the train.

Sometimes we felt the train would not come, but then we would see the distant headlight. Our anticipation grew as the train got closer. The bells rang, the lights flashed back and forth, the gates came down, and—the best part—the train whistle and the awesome, powerful sound of those thundering diesel engines. We waved and pulled our arms up and down so the engineer could wave back and give us a couple extra toots on the whistle. He always did.

Then and there, I first glimpsed the possible reality of my dream. There was just something about those trains, that distant

kids waiting at the crossing for the train

whistle calling to me. I went to bed at night, and before I fell asleep, I listened for the train blowing its whistle and rumbling through the night across the countryside. I knew it was just meant to be an important part of my life.

In 1971, I graduated from high school ready to venture out into the so-called dog-eat-dog world to find my very first job. It was kind of scary. I had no idea what to expect or even exactly what I wanted to do. I became anxious one hot summer day in July with several interviews. I had to call my dad to come pick me up in town because I didn't feel well. He said I just had a case of the nerves and that it would pass.

When we got home, I went to my room and lay down to rest. Dad later said to me, "You know, Toots (the nickname my Uncle Roy gave me because I often made a gesture with my arm like I was tooting a train whistle), you don't have to find a job the same day you graduate. Take your time, think about what you might like to do, and go from there." I took his advice, and I settled down.

Every day, I checked the help wanted ads in the newspaper to see if anything would jump out at me. I saw an ad for a local taxi service. I had my full license at seventeen and was almost eighteen. I gave it a go, and I got hired by the local taxicab service. It was a family-owned-and-operated business.

Susie at ten in 1963, top, and at high-school graduation in 1971

The owners trained me, and I got the Class 4 license I needed, assigned me a van, and off I went.

I really liked the job. It mostly involved daily contracted pickups, not flag-down strangers off the side of the road. I felt safe.

One day, my boss, Jimmy, the owner, said he had a special job for me. He said they just got awarded a new contract with the local railroad. He said we would pick up crews at the Bison Railroad Yard office and take them to the trains. As we dropped them off, we would pick up inbound crews and take them to a hotel in downtown Buffalo to rest.

I loved those trains all my life, so I felt right at home accepting the job with a great big smile.

The next day, I had to go to the railroad yard office to pick up an outbound crew, take the guys to the train, pick up a crew from the inbound train, and take them to the hotel. As I drove into the railroad yard for the first time, I saw trains and locomotives everywhere. What an awesome sight. I could smell diesel fumes in the air. I could hear the high-pitched whine of

Susie and railroad crew in the Bison Railroad Yard, 1976; including Engineer Stanley "Steve" Balon, left, Susie's adopted grandfather and mentor

turbocharged diesel engines, and I felt a slight vibration through the ground.

Oh, yes. I felt right at home. Yes, I did.

I worked my way up the gravel road to the yard office to pick up the crew, right there, ready and waiting for me. They seemed nice, and I bonded with them immediately because of my enthusiastic love for trains. We had friendly conversations, and I felt comfortable.

After I worked several years with the taxi company, the owners lost the railroad contract to a lower bidder, Blue Bird Coach Lines, a bus company out of Buffalo. I hired over at Blue Bird so I could stay with the railroad crews. During those years, certain train crews really got to know me. They encouraged me to write a letter to the railroad about hiring. They said times were changing that, even though I was a woman, my chances might be good. They said there was about to be a huge turnover as aging engineers retired and the railroad needed to hire and train future engineers.

Consolidated Rail Corporation—ConRail—began on April 1, 1976, formed when six bankrupt railroads merged: Penn Central, Central of New Jersey, Lehigh Valley, Lehigh and Hudson, Erie Lackawanna, and Reading. The goal of the corporation involved becoming a single, solvent, profitable operating railroad.

The merger created job opportunities, and the train crews continued to encourage me. I did some serious thinking and took their advice. I prepared to write a letter to ConRail to apply for a job in railroading. Sometimes, I got to climb aboard a locomotive in the yard with the crew, an experience that gave me a feeling beyond my wildest childhood dreams.

a poster announcing the creation of ConRail on April 1, 1976

One day I got the invitation of a lifetime from Engineer Sammy T. He ran Amtrak from Buffalo to Syracuse, New York. He and his crew let me ride the head end, a railroader's name for the locomotive, with them. It was a round trip job, so I knew I would be home the same day.

I realized for the very first time what a passenger engineer was all about. Wow! What an awesome job. I watched everything the

Susie ready to board a Class E8 engine out of
Buffalo with the engineer and crew

engineer did. Once, Sammy T. got up out of the engineer's seat
and told me to sit down behind the controls with my hand on
the whistle and blowing the horn.

Well, I thought I had died and gone to railroad heaven. Really.

The locomotive was an old class covered-wagon style, as
they were called back then. Today, we would call it an E8. That
locomotive had an old-time train whistle like what steam engines
had. A rope connected to the whistle from the cab ceiling hung
down with a wooden handle. The engineer pulled down on
the handle to blow the whistle. I have to admit, that was truly
awesome. I don't know for sure, but I may have been the first
twenty-three-year-old female to sit behind the controls of a
Class E8 locomotive blowing its whistle as it rolled down the
rails at a pretty good clip.

Earlier, I said I would be home the same day. Yes, and I got my very first taste of how long a day on the railroad could be. Whew! What an adventurous day. I never forgot that once-in-a-lifetime opportunity, and I never forgot Engineer Sammy Tabone.

ConRail locomotive 6799 in new colors on April 1, 1976

Learning about Railroad Work

For some time, I worked for Blue Bird Coach Lines and remained close with the railroad crews who kept me informed of railroad changes and opportunities.

Throughout the 1970s, crew members encouraged and supported me during those years. I adopted an engineer named Stanley "Steve" Balon as my grandfather. He lived in Depew, New York, near where I lived and only twelve miles from where I grew up in Orchard Park.

Steve worked out of the Bison Yard. Through him, I obtained knowledge of railroading. He gave me his own books to study about airbrake, rules of the signal system, railroad definitions and terms, and diesel locomotives and their operation. From studying the books, I could identify an engine type, its parts, its horsepower, and other details. Steve was near retirement age from ConRail after thirty-three years with the Erie-Lackawanna Railroad.

Sometimes, Steve sneaked me aboard his locomotive and taught me as if I were his apprentice. As Steve and his crew members encouraged me and believed in my ability to do the job, they circulated a petition among 123 railroad workers in all fields to support me in my intended effort to find employment as a ConRail fireman and, eventually, engineer.

I began by visiting my local state employment office, where I learned no railroad jobs were available in the Buffalo area. Further discussion discouraged me for being female and a non-veteran. I left the employment office feeling I had accomplished nothing in terms of hiring with the railroad.

The following day, I told Steve and the railroad crews about my visit to the state employment office and the disappointing results. They encouraged me to write directly to ConRail personnel officials. Steve gave me an address in Philadelphia.

The next day, pen in hand, I sat down at a small desk in the quietness of my bedroom and began to write to express my thoughts to ConRail. I have always believed in the power of the pen, and it always felt that my heart did the writing. I asked about being hired as a fireman and how to become a locomotive engineer. I told about the results of my visit to the employment office and how disappointed I was. I expressed my willingness to relocate anywhere ConRail had a hiring need for the position of fireman.

When I finished, I read and reread my thoughts. Then I put the letter into an envelope, sealed it, stamped it, and walked out to the mailbox where I deposited the envelope and put up the flag.

I had accomplished the hardest part. All I had to do was wait for a response.

After several weeks that seemed like an eternity, with me anxiously checking the mail every day, a response came. When

I saw the words "Consolidated Rail Corporation," my heart felt like it would stop. I was afraid to open it. I ran into the house, sat down, looked at it, and held it. Then, I thought, "Here goes."

I slowly opened it and began to read a letter from H. D. Good, the ConRail personnel manager.

CONRAIL

January 24, 1977

Ms. Susan L. Gaglia
48 Beverly Drive
Depew, NY   14043

Dear Ms. Gaglia:

Your letter dated November 30, 1976 and post marked January 6, 1977, concerning your interest in being employed as a fireman is welcome because it has given me the opportunity to explain our position on the matter.

First let me assure you that Conrail is interested in qualified women workers as you put it and in fact we do have a woman working as a fireman at this time. Therefore you need not be concerned that you would be deprived of the employment you seek because of your sex.

You mention that you have filed applications with several New York State Employment offices and that you have reason to believe you will not be referred for employment because you are not a veteran. Under the circumstances you may care to register your complaint with James F. Masterson, Upstate Area Director, Department of Labor State of New York, Room 558, Building 12 State Campus, Albany, NY   12240. A representative of our department will be meeting with him very soon and he will be informed that the policy you have described is not to be followed where Conrail is concerned.

Again, let me assure that if the opportunity presents itself in the future for you to be considered for employment as a fireman you will be evaluated in terms of your ability to meet our requirements and the fact that you are a woman will in no way be a deterent. Unfortunately we have not hired any firemen in the Buffalo area in almost six years and we do not anticipate a need which will offer you a fireman opportunity in the near future.

I hope this letter has helped you understand our position on the employment of women and non-veterans and I thank you again for writing to me.

Sincerely,

H. D. Good, Manager-
Employment and Personnel Practices

CONSOLIDATED RAIL CORPORATION SIX PENN CENTER PLAZA PHILADELPHIA, PA 19104

a letter from ConRail about personnel policies and women

I was somewhat pleased with what I read. The letter encouraged me with the explanation about where ConRail stood in the hiring of women and veterans. The letter, signed by a personnel executive, states that ConRail looked forward to hiring women for positions of fireman or engineer when openings occurred. To qualify, I would have to meet ConRail's requirements through interviews and pre-employment testing.

It felt like a good start in order to understand what it would take for me to capture my dream.

Qualifying for Railroad Work

A month later, I got another letter from Mr. Good. The letter says that the company is impressed with the strength of my interest in becoming a fireman.

In the letter, Mr. Good reminds me of informing me in his previous letter that ConRail did not anticipate hiring for firemen or engineers near Buffalo, but that if I were willing to relocate at my own expense, I would be considered. Mr. Good says that ConRail wanted to be sure that women had every opportunity to obtain positions traditionally held by men. "We are especially interested in increasing the number of women who may become engineers," Mr. Good writes.

He asks that I let him know if I would be interested in working elsewhere in the Northeast if positions opened.

I felt that ConRail knew my sincere interest in getting a fair chance to be hired. Seven months later, in October, I learned I would be informed when firemen positions opened when W. W. Hickey, assistant personnel manager, asked me to contact him because ConRail wanted to know where I would be willing to relocate.

CONRAIL

February 4, 1977

Ms. Susan L. Gaglia
48 Beverly Drive
Depew, NY 14043

Dear Ms. Gaglia:

Your recent letter impressed us greatly with the
strength of your interest in becoming a fireman.
From what you wrote, however, we concluded that
your interest was limited to employment in the
area where you now live.

As my reply to you stated, opportunities in your
area in the near future are not likely to be available, simply because we do not anticipate having
any vacancies there. However, we may need firemen
for training as engineers in other areas at a much
earlier time.

One of our purposes is to be sure that women have
every opportunity to obtain the kinds of positions
they have not traditionally held. We are especially
interested in increasing the number of women who may
become engineers. Therefore, it will be appreciated
if you will let us know whether you would be interested in working in other parts of the Northeast if
positions become available and, if so, whether there
are any areas where you would be unwilling to be
employed.

If you are interested in working elsewhere, we would
arrange to have you apply at Buffalo at the appropriate
time so that we could determine whether you qualify
without your having to travel. If you qualify, it would,
of course, then be up to you to relocate on your own to
the point where you would be employed.

I am looking forward to hearing from you.

Sincerely,

H. D. Good, Manager
Employment and Personnel Practices

CONSOLIDATED RAIL CORPORATION   SIX PENN CENTER PLAZA   PHILADELPHIA, PA 19104

an encouraging letter from ConRail

As my correspondence with ConRail unfolded, I grew
excited, and so did the railroad crews, who were behind me all
the way.

I received a letter in November, 1977, from S. W. Seeman,
director of personnel, explaining that ConRail hired

locomotive firemen when vacancies open and that, in turn, firemen become engineers after successful completion of the ConRail engineman training program. The letter states that someone from the company would contact me when vacancies opened in the Pennsylvania or western New York area. He says he hopes I will apply and qualify.

CONRAIL

November 23, 1977

Miss Susan L. Gaglia
48 Beverly Drive
Depew, NY 14043

Dear Miss Gaglia:

Because of some reassignment of responsibilities, your most recent letter about becoming a locomotive engineer has come to me.

As I think you know, we hire locomotive firemen when we have vacancies and they, in turn, become engineers after successful completion of our Engineman Training Program. When we next have firemen vacancies any place in Pennsylvania or in western New York, we will contact you directly to arrange your application at the point where new employees are needed.

I hope that an opportunity for you to apply will occur soon, that you do apply, and that you are successful in qualifying.

Sincerely,

S. W. Seeman, Director
Agreement Personnel

an invitation to apply for a job with ConRail

A letter arrived for me in December, 1977, from the ConRail regional personnel manager, W. L. Holland. Mr. Holland's letter announces ConRail's recruitment of candidates for fireman vacancies in the Reading, Pennsylvania, area. The letter says that my interest had come to Mr. Holland's attention.

He says that he had arranged an appointment for me to meet with his assistant, E. B. Ruark, to complete an application, interview, and testing. I was to meet Mr. Ruark at 30th Street Station in Philadelphia on December 16, 1977.

Although I was excited, I was not pleased. The letter dated December 8 arrived on December 14, allowing me only two days to get the money I needed and make arrangements for a flight out of Buffalo and to schedule the flight. Engineer Steve lent me the money, booked my first flight, and saw me off from Greater Buffalo International Airport on December 16.

I was excited but overwhelmed and somewhat scared. It was my very first time in the air, but when I calmed my nerves, I began to enjoy looking out the window at white, billowing, fluffy clouds. I loved the sound of those jet engines, and soon I was okay.

I arrived at 30th Street Station and met with Mr. Ruark. I filled out the application for employment. Mr. Ruark interviewed me and took me into a quiet room to take a pre-employment test, and that was it.

My flight was scheduled the next morning, and I stayed at a nearby hotel. I felt I was growing up fast. I felt so alone in a huge, unfamiliar city without knowing what direction my life was going.

Morning came, and I boarded my flight home to Buffalo. Steve was right there waiting for me. He truly became my hero of a grandfather. I could not have done it without him.

CONRAIL

December 8, 1977

Miss Susan L. Gaglia
48 Beverly Drive
Depew, N. Y. 14043

Dear Miss Gaglia:

Copies of your recent correspondence with Mr. S. W. Seeman,
Director Agreement Personnel, have come to my attention.

We are presently in the process of recruiting candidates for
existing fireman vacancies in the Reading, Pennsylvania area.
Because of your particular interest, I have taken the liberty
of arranging an appointment for you with my Assistant, E. B.
Ruark, so that a proper application, interview and testing may be
completed.

Please arrange to report to my office, Room 209, 30th Street
Station, Philadelphia, Pa., 19104 at 1:00 P.M., on December 16,
1977 in order for you to discuss the probabilities of your
employment with Mr. Ruark.

If you should have any questions you may contact me. My
telephone number is (215) 594-3562. Likewise, you may reach
Mr. Ruark at his number (215) 594-3140.

Very truly yours,

W. L. Holland
Regional Personnel Manager

410 30th Street Station
Philadelphia, Pa. 19104

an appointment for an interview

Mr. Ruark told me I should receive results in about three
weeks. It felt good to be home, and I was ready to celebrate the
holidays with my family.

A Disappointment

The Christmas holidays arrived, and the whole family was at our house. Oh, how I loved seeing everyone—aunts, uncles, cousins—it was just the happiest time of the year. I remember those times like it was yesterday.

I invited Engineer Steve, as he was a widower living alone in his home. He and my dad had much to talk about. They discussed my wish to become a railroad engineer, the letters I wrote and received, and my quick trip to Philadelphia for the interview and testing. Everyone was excited and even in awe, as I was, too.

The holidays passed, and the new year arrived. I checked the mail every day, waiting for a response from ConRail.

I put on my coat and boots and shuffled through newly fallen snow to the mailbox one bitter cold day during the first week of the new year. There it was: the letter from ConRail.

Excited but nervous, I got back into the house where it was warm and sat down in the living room, where I paused before opening the letter. It starts positive with a "thank you for your interest in becoming a fireman for ConRail." It goes on to say that ConRail selects individuals best qualified for training based on a variety of considerations.

I was okay with what I read until the third paragraph, which says, "I regret that you were not selected inasmuch as you did not successfully pass the pre-employment tests which were administered to you on December 16." Mr. Holland signed the letter.

How can I explain what I felt at the devastating news? A horrible feeling of emptiness came over me. My heart hurt. I could not hold back tears. I was choking.

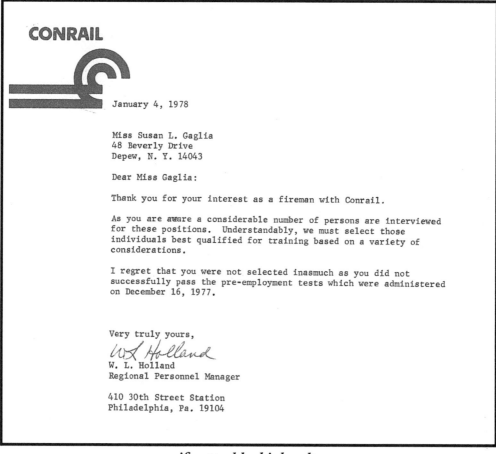

CONRAIL

January 4, 1978

Miss Susan L. Gaglia
48 Beverly Drive
Depew, N. Y. 14043

Dear Miss Gaglia:

Thank you for your interest as a fireman with Conrail.

As you are aware a considerable number of persons are interviewed for these positions. Understandably, we must select those individuals best qualified for training based on a variety of considerations.

I regret that you were not selected inasmuch as you did not successfully pass the pre-employment tests which were administered on December 16, 1977.

Very truly yours,

W. L. Holland
Regional Personnel Manager

410 30th Street Station
Philadelphia, Pa. 19104

as if zapped by high voltage

I was glad I was alone. I felt like I had been zapped by high voltage. I was frozen and couldn't move or speak. It was as if I were trying to run away from myself but couldn't.

I went to my room and lay down. I did not want to talk to anyone.

A few days of deep depression lingered in me, and then, my true-grit spirit arose. My belief in the power of the pen returned, and I began to write again. I gathered up all the ConRail letters I had and put them together with a cover letter addressed to the top dog, the president and chief executive officer of ConRail, Richard D. Spence.

I poured out my heartfelt thoughts and disappointment in ConRail and his personnel people. I told him what I had been through to get hired. I explained the dream I had to become a railroad engineer to the best of my ability and that I needed only one person to believe in me and give me another chance to prove that I could qualify to be a fireman so that I could become an engineer.

I was young and had a lot of good fight in me. Failure had never been a part of me, and I wanted to go another round. I had plenty of support from family and especially from Steve and the railroad crews, who agreed that I should send along the petition they had all signed in November.

After enclosing the petition with the letters, I sealed the large envelope, addressed it to Mr. Spence, and off it went to Philadelphia.

I had no idea what to expect.

Good News

About six weeks after I sent off my letter to the top, I got a response. In a letter dated March 15, 1978, Betsy Robinson, assistant vice-president of personnel for ConRail, expresses understanding of my disappointment at not qualifying to be a fireman. She explains the importance of pre-employment tests and why they are administered. She says (and you've gotta love this part, because I did):

> Because of our strong interest in increasing the number of women engineers, we are arranging another opportunity for you to qualify. Mr. W. W. Hickey will contact you for retesting in Buffalo. I hope you are successful.

In late March, W. W. Hickey, ConRail personnel manager, contacted me by phone and set a date for me to be retested with him in the Buffalo office. I met Mr. Hickey several days later. He administered the test, scored it in my presence, smiled, shook my hand congratulated me, and said, "Pack your bags. You're off to Philadelphia."

On April 12, 1978, I received the following:

CONRAIL

April 12, 1978

Miss Susan L. Gaglia
48 Beverly Drive
Depew, New York 14043

Dear Miss Gaglia:

I am glad to be able to tell you that we are
prepared to employ you as a fireman, subject
only to your passing the regular preemployment
physical examination. Our Regional Personnel
Manager at Philadelphia will contact you shortly
to inform you as to the next step.

Best wishes for success in realizing your ambition
to become an engineer.

Sincerely,

S. W. Seeman, Director
Agreement Personnel

SWS:gmr

315 Six Penn Center
Philadelphia, PA 19104

soon to be a fireman

Things were looking up. My fight, dogged determination, and perseverance pulled me through.

The next letter from ConRail signed by W. B. Suhirie, regional road foreman and dated May 15, 1978, informs me that ConRail was hiring firemen to become engineers in the company's eastern region including Trenton, New Jersey; Philadelphia; Wilmington, Delaware; and Baltimore. I could choose where I wanted to relocate to begin my railroad career. I chose Wilmington.

Through all this, I must admit, I was tired and somewhat scared. It was the beginning of an unusual new life in a different world.

I packed my bags and said my goodbyes.

Off I went to start my new life alone in Wilmington. Once or twice I asked myself, "Do I really know what I am doing?"

I soon realized I would be living my dream and everything would be okay.

Off to Philadelphia.

My older sister Bonnie and I packed up my 1969 Chevy Malibu and headed to the big city of Philadelphia. Bonnie was two years older and always protective of me. She did not want me to go away from home alone.

As we traveled the highway in some disbelief of what was actually happening, Bonnie felt unsettled at times. I knew she thought she would lose her little sister, but I also knew she felt pride in my achievement.

We arrived in Philadelphia at 30th Street Station, where I met with the ConRail personnel manager. He gave me what I needed with directions to Edgemoor Yard in Wilmington, Delaware, which would become my home depot. Again, my sister and I jumped into the Malibu and headed to Delaware. We arrived in Wilmington and located the Edgemoor Yard, drove in, and checked it out.

The yardmaster and crew dispatcher expected me. They welcomed me and gave me directions to a nearby motel that would be my temporary home until I could find an apartment and get settled.

I had nothing but my car, some clothes, and a few hundred dollars. I would have to stretch that until my first paycheck. It was like camping out or roughing it, known as self-survival.

Susie's sister Bonnie in 1978

The next day my sister boarded an airport shuttle and returned home to Buffalo. I can honestly say that day was the hardest day of our entire lives. We clung onto each other in tears. She felt she was losing her baby sister, and I felt totally alone in a strange place with a long journey ahead of me to prove I could achieve my dream, that I could and would become a railroad locomotive engineer and that I would become one of the best.

My First Day on the Railroad

It was my first day on the railroad, and I was excited. I was also very nervous. I made my way over to the Edgemoor Yard office, where I was to meet up with Harold Lee, an engineer everyone called JW because they considered him the John Wayne of the railroad.

I would work a light-engines job from three in the afternoon to eleven at night. I thought, "Wow."

Locomotives sounded like my kind of job. I arrived at the yard office ahead of time because I was always a believer in being on time. Dad taught me that.

The engineer had not arrived yet, so I introduced myself to others there. I sat and talked with Oscar Eller, the crew dispatcher. Oscar did other jobs, too, but today filled in at the desk. He explained his job and told me how firemen and engineers work extra boards or lists as they're called. Those with regular jobs didn't have to be called, but extras did. This light-engines job qualified as a regular set-timed job. No need to be called.

Oscar explained to me that if I got bumped off the regular job by a senior railroader, I could bid on any jobs advertised or open or that I might have to work the extra board. Oscar explained that the extra board consists of a log of different jobs and that I could be called in as little as six hours with a two-hour time window to arrive for that job.

I understood that if I worked an eight-hour job, been up, say, for fourteen hours, and turned up first out on the extra list with three jobs showing, then I'd better get my rest, because in six hours, I could get a call.

Working the extra board required discipline in getting sufficient rest in case of a call.

Engineer JW arrived, and oh, boy. He really did look like John Wayne and just as big. He walked and talked like him, too. I took to him right away. I was always a big fan of the legendary John Wayne.

JW took one look at me (all four feet, eleven and three-quarters inches), smiled, and said, "Why you're as cute as a bug's ear."

He asked if I was ready to learn how to be an engineer.

I said, "Yes, sir!"

It seemed that he took to me right away, too, because he began telling the guys, "Look at my new fireman." Railroaders used that old name back in the days of steam. Now they would say "apprentice engineer."

It seemed as though JW really enjoyed letting everyone know I would be working with him. He took me under his wing and called me "Precious."

I heard that other railroaders respected JW as one hell of an engineer. I felt safe and eager to learn from the best.

JW got his orders from the yard office and said, "C'mon, Precious. Let's go."

We walked out the back door to the engine house pit. Wow! Locomotives everywhere humming. I could feel the ground vibrating under my feet and smell the strong odor of diesel fumes. My heart pounded, and I felt right at home. I knew I was off to a good start. I felt comfortable.

I tagged along behind JW, who stood 6-feet, 4 inches and about 230 pounds with me at 4-feet, 11¾ inches and 115 pounds.

Sometimes, JW stopped and waited for me to catch up. He looked out for my safety.

We approached three huge, strange looking black engines. They were enormous! I never saw such an engine.

I wasn't sure about it. Then, JW said, "Precious, you are about to climb aboard the famous Class GG1 electric locomotive, the pride of the Pennsylvania Railroad."

I had expected something different, as I grew up in diesel country. Now I worked in both diesel and electrified railroad territory, known as the Northeast Corridor. This stretch of railroad runs between Washington, DC, to New York City and New Haven and all points in between. Electric class engines in the Northeast Corridor use a pantograph, located on top of the locomotive, and running along an overhead, eleven-thousand volt catenary wire system. I felt very uneasy around all that high voltage. I didn't like it at all.

JW sensed my fear and discomfort, but he set me at ease and explained to me how to be safe. I soon learned to respect the electric engines and overhead catenary lines.

We had to climb aboard the steel stirrup ladder into the engine cab compartment. When I stood beside that huge engine, the

*Susie training behind the controls of
Pennsylvania Class GG1 locomotive 4800, now in the
Railroad Museum of Pennsylvania in Strasburg*

first stirrup was chest high. JW put his hands together and made a booster step for me, and up I went with JW right behind me.

We entered the cab of the GG1, a really old engine and rough looking. JW began to talk me through everything so I would become familiar and comfortable with the engine, but all the time I thought quietly, "Oh, please don't make me run it!"

JW got our orders from the train dispatcher to leave the yard and proceed to the main line. We were going to Philadelphia. I wanted to learn. I watched everything JW did, and I listened to everything he said. That's a key word here, *listened*.

He was really somethin'. We started to roll. This was getting exciting.

We got more orders from the tower operator to enter the main line and proceed to Philadelphia. We rolled at about fifty miles per hour. Chills ran through me. The awesome sound of that powerful huge steel locomotive impressed me, and so did JW.

For the next two months, I remained on the job with JW, and I must say, I had a great and exhilarating learning experience. I will never forget the day the John Wayne of the railroad said to me, "Precious, put those books away. I'm gonna teach you how to run a train by the seat of your pants." And, by golly, he did just that.

I was off to a good start, and I knew I would be okay.

Engineer Harold Lee, called JW as
the John Wayne of the railroad, who mentored Susie from
1978 to 1979

Runaway Engine

After a couple of months working steady with JW and feeling comfortable, it happened! It was my turn to learn all about the railroad seniority game. I got my first bump off by a senior fireman, which forced me to look for another open job or a younger-in-seniority fireman to bump off a job I might want. I liked that option. Made me feel like I wasn't quite on the bottom of the totem pole.

As Oscar explained earlier to me, being a low seniority railroader sometimes forced an employee to work an extra board, which entitled that person to work a variety of jobs with different senior engineers and crews. I found the experience very good and smart for all around learning.

I worked the extra board for several months. Then I put a bid in for an open 7 AM to 3 PM hostler job at the engine house, which I felt pleased to be awarded. The railroad term hostler signifies a person moving locomotives around the engine house to get them serviced and ready to go on a run.

At seven in the morning on a beautiful, sunny summer day, I worked on my new job. So far, so good. I mean, at least I had my morning coffee and breakfast sandwich.

The job required me to climb aboard locomotives and move them to and from the engine-house pit for checking, servicing, and fueling.

Engineers on inbound trains sometimes cut engines away from trains and brought them straight to the engine house pit and left them. That's where I came into play as a hostler moving engines.

I worked on my own. I did not have a senior engineer to follow around or lean on. I felt a little nervous at first, but I jumped right in with both feet, and I was fine. I had enough basic training with different class locomotives, so I knew about the set-up of units and how to separate and join them together by large cables attached to the front and rear of the locomotive.

The day was going along very well, and I felt good about the job. I especially liked it, because I was my own boss.

The hours moved along fast, and I took a short lunch break. While I was taking lunch, an inbound engineer brought a Class GG1 engine to the engine house and left it for service. The GG1 could be set up to operate at either end of the locomotive, to pull in either direction.

I finished my lunch. I had to couple or link the GG1 to another engine to save time. Sometimes, I might couple six or seven engines together at a time.

On that day, the move required me only to take one engine and couple it to the GG1 left by the incoming engineer. For that purpose, I operated a Class GP38, a general purpose engine with less horsepower. As I went to make the slow forward coupling, the engine couplers did not completely line up, and when I bumped, they did not latch together. The GG1 forward engine started to roll away.

Susie working as a hostler at the Edgmoor Enginehouse in 1978

The incoming engineer had not set the brake, and that allowed the engine to drift forward. There was just enough grade to keep it rolling, heading toward the south end switch leading into the yard where engines enter and exit from the engine house.

I must admit, I felt a sense of panic. I set the brake on the engine I operated and quickly climbed down and ran as fast as I could through sand, jumping over yard debris such as old railroad-tie switch plates, visible safety hazards.

It felt like an eternity to catch up to the runaway engine. I reached out to grab the ladder rung, but it dragged me along because I couldn't get my foot up into the stirrup. Imagine a tiny woman trying to stop a three-hundred-thousand-pound locomotive.

It didn't work.

I made a second effort, and this time, I got my knees in the bottom stirrup, and yeow! That hurt! Bone on steel. Get the picture? It's just what I had to do, but not without considerable pain.

I quickly climbed aboard to find the controls set up on the opposite end. Go figure. I had to work my way through the hot, scary compartment of the engine to the other end in order to stop it. I finally got it stopped, but not before it ran through the south end switch and derailed.

I hadn't caught my breath nor gathered my composure when I realized what had happened. I thought, "Oh, no! My first derailment, and so soon. I'm going to get fired."

I got on the radio and called the yardmaster to tell him what had happened. He told me to stay put and that help would be on the way.

My heart still pounding, I waited soaked in sweat. I couldn't believe what had happened.

Soon men from the engine house and shops arrived. The yardmaster told me I would remain on the engine and follow instructions from the men on the ground, that we were going to rerail the engine.

The rerailing procedure took a while. It consisted of positioning metal tie plates and wooden blocks just so under the wheels.

The Class GG1 locomotive had twelve traction motors, twelve wheels, and two pony trucks. It weighed about three hundred thousand pounds.

Rerailing the huge locomotive involved an amazing process. The men qualified as professionals in every sense of the word. I was truly impressed.

I did not know how to do the job of rerailing, but I learned quickly, thanks to expert instruction. The men said I did great. I was a natural! I felt so proud. I mean, really proud.

It didn't seem like they made a big deal out of it. They said, "Hey, it happens!"

That was my first frightening experience on the railroad. An assigned 7 AM to 3 PM hostler job at the engine house ended up an extremely exhausting twelve-hour day.

Whew!

Sudden Illness

On October 5, 1978, after six long months of working a variety of jobs with different engineers and crews, I took a few days off to rest and get other things done.

I learned that when working for the railroad, you are the railroad, and your time and life become all railroad. When you're called, you go. Hours turn into days, days into nights. You eat, sleep, and breathe railroad, and that's the life of a dedicated railroad engineer.

I had no social life, no family life. Holidays were just another day. That's just the way it was. The job of a railroad engineer or conductor is not for everyone. You are a special breed. You are proud to work for the railroad. It becomes a lifelong bond.

On that beautiful fall day, at home enjoying my day off, I suddenly felt sick. I had stomach and abdominal pain and discomfort. I thought, "Oh, it's just a bad case of bloat and trapped gas," so I lay down hoping it would pass. It did, so I continued doing what needed to get done.

I went to bed around eleven and woke up around three in the morning in terrible pain, soaked in sweat, my body shaking. My teeth chattered uncontrollably. I knew something was terribly wrong. I began to panic, thinking the worst, asking myself, "What's happening to me? Am I going to die right here by myself?"

I had only been in Delaware six months working on the railroad. I didn't know whom to call. My family lived hundreds of miles away in Buffalo. JW lived fifty miles away, so I called my crew dispatcher, Oscar, who lived just up the road from me.

Yes. I know what you're thinking. 911 would have been a good choice, true. But, hey. At age twenty-five, what did I know about pain and dying?

Soon, Oscar and his wife arrived and immediately wrapped me in a blanket and took me to Saint Francis Hospital in Wilmington. The hospital people rushed me into emergency surgery with a possible ruptured appendix. I went out cold. I didn't know anything.

After five-and-a-half hours in surgery, I went into recovery. When I awoke, I didn't remember much. Nurses cared for me. I was hooked up to mysterious different things, and I was frightened.

The surgeon came to see me. He said I was a lucky girl. He said they found a leaking abscess on the lower colon just below my appendix. They said it was about to burst and would have killed me.

I saw Oscar and JW there watching over me. They had contacted my family.

I remained in the hospital for six days with drainage tubes up my nose and other tubes down my throat into my stomach. Oh, that was so uncomfortable. I kept asking the nurses, "How

Susie's parents, Raymond and Pearl Gaglia, in 1978

much longer do these tubes have to stay in?" I wanted them out! I literally counted the hours each day, and like my dear mother, I had an iron will and true grit. I was tough, and I knew I would get through it.

On the seventh day, they released me from the hospital. I had some serious recovering to do before jumping back on the trains. My mom and dad traveled down from Buffalo to care for me during my dad's thirteen-week time off from Bethlehem Steel.

It took me about eight weeks to recover fully.

I returned to work in December, still favoring my right side where muscles were cut and a thick, eight-inch scar remained.

It took me a while to get back into the swing of things, but I managed. I got lucky and hooked up again with JW on an 11 PM to 7 AM light-engines job. That eight-hour job always turned into twelve-hour days. JW looked out for me. That was a blessing, and I was able to stay on that job for several months.

After I spent several months with JW, the old seniority railroad game began again. I got bumped off the job by a senior fireman. I decided to try my hand in passenger service for Amtrak.

Amtrak then used ConRail crews to run its trains on the Northeast Corridor high-speed railroad between Washington and New York: 226 miles at 80 to 120 miles per hour.

I made a bid on a job as fireman or apprentice engineer on the *Night Owl*, Train 178-67 out of Washington to New York. I would work with an engineer named Tom Staley, a veteran with years of experience. I took to him right off, and we remained a team for several months at a time. I really liked that job. It was high speed railroading at its best. I felt like a real high roller.

Engineer Tom Staley on the Amtrak Northeast Corridor

The job required me to deadhead, a railroad term for hitching a free ride to work, in this case, by train. I would drive to Wilmington Station and hop aboard a scheduled train that would get me to Washington terminal in time for my job.

The *Night Owl* ran out of Washington around 3:20 PM and arrived in New York at 8:30 PM. We took rest at a hotel, then worked our scheduled train back to Washington, departing around 3:20 AM and arriving in Washington around 9 AM.

Susie on a Class E60 engine during a **Night Owl** *run from Washington*

The job required me to work four trips on and one off. It was a real sweet job, my all-time favorite. My only fear was having a senior fireman bump me off. I managed to hold on for a good while: long enough to learn how to run a high-speed passenger train safely and on time with a regular engineer who took the time to teach me everything he knew.

Sometimes, Tom let me know he was proud without letting me get a big head.

The Road to Engineer

After going to work with ConRail on May 26, 1978, and working a year on several jobs as a fireman, I planned to prepare for the engineman training program about to begin in mid May, 1979 and run for seven weeks through mid July.

The syllabus included instruction in duties; identification of locomotive components; introduction to electricity, generators, and high voltage circuits; airbrake systems; low voltage systems; locomotive operation; troubleshooting; running gear; and inspections and reports.

This is what I'd been waiting for. This was the main reason I chose to be a railroader, to achieve my All-American Dream of becoming a locomotive engineer.

The day arrived. The only female and more than ready to get started, I went to class as one of fifteen candidates chosen.

Although always a quiet, shy person, on that special day, I became an instant friend and buddy with another young fireman trainee named RJ. Railroaders often identified themselves by their first and middle initials—just a tradition, I guess. My initials are SL, not exactly the right tone. So I ended up with other nicknames like Shortline, Little Bit, or Susie Q. Senior railroaders like JW called me Precious. I found that nickname way too girly for me, but I accepted it with a little grin.

RJ reminded me of my childhood friend, PJ, who lived across the street where I grew up and who chased trains with me.

RJ and I hit it off and became classroom buddies. We relied on each other to get through the seven weeks of training school.

I got a good night's sleep and reported to class at eight in the morning. In the small classroom, desks were similar to those of my high school days. I chose my desk to the far left near the windows in the front row with RJ right behind me. I vaguely remember others in the class.

I guess once I found a buddy, I was all set. No need to look any further. RJ felt the same way, so for us, engineer school had officially begun. We were ready.

The instructors came in and introduced themselves. Naturally, and I knew this was coming, they asked each one of us to stand up and introduce ourselves to the class. Because I'm shy, I always hated that.

The instructors lectured us on what to expect for the next seven weeks. They gave us classroom handouts and books to use for training: they were ours to keep. In those days before computers and tablets, I immediately started a three-ring notebook with dividers and sheet protectors. I was always good at neatness and organizing my schoolwork. During my school years, my teachers often complimented me about it.

We had a lot to learn in just seven weeks, and our instructors told us not to fall behind.

The first informational day came to an end. RJ and I walked out together to our cars, chatted a while, and headed to our respective homes. We all headed home, but not without homework. A lot of homework.

I had recently settled in a small apartment in New Castle, Delaware. My desk was my kitchen table, and that's where I did all my homework.

The first week of school ended, and it was not easy. It would surely get more difficult as days and weeks passed.

Two more weeks passed, and we were into our fourth week of training. The assignments got harder. Both RJ and I felt as if our brains were burning out and with no more room to fit any more. At times, I fell asleep at the kitchen table with my head on my books, and other times I wept from stress and brain overload. Training to become a locomotive engineer was extremely difficult.

At times, RJ and I studied together. We sometimes doubted we would make it through. In class, I passed some quizzes and written tests and barely passed others. I kept a notebook with all my test scores, and I still have that book. It's my personal nostalgia.

As the instructor handed out another book, I smiled because I remembered what Engineer JW said to me one day about putting those books away, that he was going to teach me how to "run a train by the seat of my pants," and here they were teaching us modern day railroading from a book.

My opinion? That old-time railroading is hard to beat.

More days and weeks of nonstop, grueling learning went by, and I kept passing the tests. RJ had a little trouble, but I helped him through. At times, he lost confidence that he could do it. I listened to him, encouraged him, and helped restore his confidence in his dream. He went home feeling better.

The school training wound down, and the time for our finals arrived. The night before, I quickly browsed through my well-organized notes and material, but not too much, because too much repeated study caused me to burn out and become nervous. I wanted to feel calm and confident, and I was ready to reach for my dream. I was more than ready to become a locomotive engineer for the railroad.

On the last day of training class, the time came to take the final written exam. The instructor passed out papers one by one and wished us good luck. We began. You could hear a pin drop.

I had always had a little trouble with comprehension, and it took me a little longer to finish, but when I was confident, I put down my pencil and handed in my completed exam.

RJ and I went to get a cold soda pop and a genuine, mouthwatering Philly cheese steak grinder to talk and unwind. It was a very tiring day, but it was a good day.

An instructor would give Part Two of the final exam, a practical, the following day outside on the locomotives. I would have to identify engine parts, make a total inspection of the equipment, start and shut down the locomotive, and perform an airbrake test while describing what each handle position does.

And, of course, #1 priority: *safety* at all times.

It was intense with no room for mistakes. The instructor remained quiet and followed me around with a clipboard, watching everything I did or didn't do.

This was my time to shine, and I did all the talking and teaching. That late July day took its toll on both the instructor and me with temperatures in the mid nineties and humidity high. I don't know who wanted that day to end sooner, him or me. Whew!

*an instructor administers the practical exam to a
well-prepared Susie*

The day I had anticipated and worked so hard for finally arrived. We had all completed our finals, and the results were in. We met at the school with the instructors, who handed us our results and congratulated us. Our classmates congratulated us, too. RJ and I hugged for the first time. We jumped up and down like a couple of excited kids watching a train going by at a road crossing on this, the greatest day of our lives. We had earned the right to work as official railroad locomotive engineers.

A table of hors d'oeuvres and a giant cake made the occasion a celebration. Never before or since have I felt as I did that day: a very proud day indeed.

Later, some of the railroad men I worked with—like JW, Oscar, Tom, and Danny—presented me with cards and gifts. Conductor M. J. DiSanta painted a portrait of me from a photo Oscar gave him.

Susie: qualified to be an engineer

    The portrait hangs on the wall in my basement railroad room. JW gave me an HO scale model of the GG1 4935 in a wooden collector box. Danny gave me an HO scale model of an Amtrak Class E60 locomotive. Oscar gave me a railroad pocket watch, and Tom gave me a gift certificate to a local hobby shop. It was a fine celebration.

CONRAIL

This is to certify that

S. L. GAGLIA

has successfully completed the

Engineman Training Program

and is hereby promoted to

LOCOMOTIVE ENGINEER ·

VBSubrie
General Road Foreman

OCTOBER 2, 1979
Date

Engineer Instructor

Susie's certificate of completing the Engineman Training Program,
October 2, 1979

LOUISVILLE & NASHVILLE RAILROAD COMPANY

908 W. BROADWAY · LOUISVILLE, KENTUCKY 40203 · TELEPHONE (502) 587-5351

RICHARD D. SPENCE
PRESIDENT

August 7, 1980

Ms. S. L. Gaglia
29-17 Holland Circle
New Castle, Delaware 19720

Dear Susie:

        Thank you for the delightful letter, the pictures
of a very proud locomotive engineer, and for the news of
your success.

        Mrs. Butler told me of your coming by the office
while I was away. I was very sorry to have missed you
because I did recall our correspondence. I was very pleased
to learn from her that you had received your promotion and
even more happy to receive the confirmation from you.

        You are to be complimented on both the level of your
achievement and your dogged determination to get there. I
am, indeed, proud of you. I hope too that there are even
greater things ahead for you. Dedication is an essential
ingredient, both to success and to being a good railroader.
You have that quality.

        I am leaving Louisville very shortly to become
Executive Vice President-Operations for the Family Lines.
Perhaps your journeys will bring you to Jacksonville, Florida,
at some point in time. Please come by the office so I can
congratulate you in person.

                        Sincerely,

                        Richard D. Spence

an encouraging letter from Richard D. Spence,
former executive with ConRail

a portrait of Susie by Conductor M. J. DiSanta
celebrating her certification as engineer

Engineer Apprenticeship

With the seven-week engineman training class completed, it was time for apprenticeship. So: back on the trains and learning the yards and all the characteristics of the railroad where I would operate trains. Railroaders called the mandatory apprenticeship "qualifications." I would work a variety of jobs with different senior engineers who would train me and grade my performance in train handling for each job. Grading took into account attendance, safety, knowledge of the rules, signals, track speeds, engine and train operations, and proper use of dynamic braking on locomotives so equipped.

Here are a few types of trains I would work and train on:

• coal trains that transported coal from the mines to power plants

• truck trains that transported tractor trailers on flatbed railroad cars

• auto racks that transported automobiles

• stack trains that transported stacked cargo containers on flatbed railroad cars

- grain trains that transported cars loaded with grain from local feed mills
- chemical trains that transported tanker cars loaded with hazardous materials
- hopper trains that transported empty coal cars

Although apprenticeship resembled jobs I worked as a fireman for my first six months and before my promotion to engineer, information grew much deeper. I felt an even greater sense of pride and eagerness to work as a professional engineer for the railroad.

I felt proud to have earned the title of locomotive engineer.

I never forgot where it all began in my little hometown of Orchard Park, New York, growing up hearing the sound of distant train whistles, and riding my bike as a youngster to the railroad crossings to wait for the train.

Susie as an apprentice engineer with
Joe Cheseldine, senior engineer, in 1979

I could never forget the anticipation and thrill of seeing, hearing, and smelling the train as it passed by nor the thrill of waving to the engineer and getting an extra toot on the whistle. Yes, those precious memories will always be with me.

As an engineer, I wanted to keep that tradition going in me for all the kids and rail fans alongside the tracks waiting and watching for the train, taking pictures, waving to me for a wave back and extra toots on the whistle. I always remembered those times. This was my dream, and my dream became a reality, and I wanted that same dream for all those who believed as I once did.

I never forgot the time when I was a little older, maybe nineteen or so, and I approached a railroad crossing in my car. I sat there alone at the gate. I got out of the car and stood leaning on the hood waiting for the train like old times. I wanted to wave

Susie as engineer on a Class F40PH
Amtrak train in Washington in 1981

to the engineer and see if he would give an extra toot on the whistle for me.

When the train approached and the locomotives crossed over the road, the engineer outstretched his arm, waved, and tooted the whistle two or three more times.

At that exact time. I felt something so powerful in me. I raised my right arm, pointed my finger toward the engines, and said aloud, "That's gonna be me one day, Mr. Engineer, and I will carry on the tradition for you in that seat." At that moment as the train cars sped by me, I felt a chill rush through my body, and for a moment, I remained still.

Now I ran the trains, and I was the engineer, and I waved to the people and kids alongside the railroad tracks waiting for the train, anticipating a few more toots on the whistle. I, too, thought, as I had years before when I wanted to be in the engineer's seat, that someone out there would one day replace me in that very same seat.

Life as a Railroad Engineer

After about four steady months of on-the-job training, working a variety of different jobs, I fulfilled requirements and qualified over all the railroad territory in the Philadelphia division of ConRail.

I completed the engineer training program on October 2, 1979, and became a locomotive engineer. Later, in May, 1980, I would receive the official certificate in the mail. I had long awaited the arrival of that certificate of completion, and when it showed up in the mail, I remember my excitement at opening that oversized envelope.

I already had my special frame ready for it, but when I opened the envelope and pulled out the certificate, someone had folded it unevenly. The crease went right through my name. Instantly, my heart hurt. A happy, proud moment became suddenly sad. I asked myself, and I will ask you, "Who would do such a thing?"

I wanted so much to frame it, and I even tried to iron out the crease, but I couldn't, and to this day, the crease remains.

Perhaps the individual who creased my certificate has gone on to that big railroad office in the sky. The certificate, however, endures and hangs proudly in a frame on my wall in my home.

Susie, engineer on a class F40PH in Wilmington

As an engineer, I had little seniority, so I worked the engineers' extra board or list, as it's called. I got called out to work different jobs at different times with different crews.

Crews then consisted of four men or, in this case, three men and one woman: engineer, fireman, conductor, and brakeman. The crew dispatcher called me sometimes with six hours' notice and a two-hour window to get to the assigned job. Sometimes the distance from home to a job location took an hour or more for me.

Extra board work required discipline and rest. Working trains without sufficient rest could prove dangerous, as every railroader's instincts knows.

The job of a locomotive engineer carries tremendous responsibility. Plus, when working the board, when called, you go. The railroad runs 24/7, 365 days a year. True-blooded railroaders eat, sleep, breathe, and live the railroad. They become the railroad. I became the railroad.

I had no social life. I couldn't make plans and depend on them, so plans I made often ended in disappointment. On the railroad, holidays were like any other day.

People often asked if I were married. With a grin, I answered, "Yeah. To the railroad."

My time—my life—became all railroad. I honored my career, my profession. I was dedicated. I was proud to work for the railroad.

A railroad engineer lives a hard life. It's not for everyone. Once it's in your blood, though, it consumes you.

So many stories have been told about this job, this very high risk job. Engineers do not know for certain if they will reach the destination or if they will return home safely after a long run.

Susie aboard locomotive 6403
ready to leave on a run to Harrisburg

Although railroaders don't dwell on such thoughts, they know and accept the reality.

The history and stories told over the years by heroic railroad men and women reflect personal nostalgia of days lived since the beginning of the train and will live on in generations to come.

The life of a railroad engineer exhausted me both mentally and physically. Sometimes, despite committing myself to discipline and sufficient rest, I started a job I thought would turn out routine—a nice, normal, easy one, but it ended up going on for hours and hours. I thought it would never end.

The law limited an engineer to twelve hours of actually operating a train during a single shift, but the job did not end with that twelve hours. Sometimes it turned into fourteen- and sixteen-hour days.

I got so tired sometimes that I couldn't wait to get to the hotel and hit the bed or get home and hit the bed. It seemed like bed came to be my favorite place. Sometimes, I awakened and momentarily did not know where I was, hotel or home. I felt disoriented, a strange sensation triggered by pure exhaustion.

Sometimes I took a rest at the hotel while waiting for the call to my return trip. Sometimes that went well, I got my rest, and I got called in reasonable time for my homebound train. Other times, I waited and waited hour after hour, becoming very restless. The hotels where I stayed were no resorts and I got bored and sometimes over-rested.

My train home sometimes got delayed after hours and hours of waiting, and the crew would then get called to deadhead home, usually by shuttle van at no personal expense but sometimes by free taxi or train. Sometimes such a ride grew long and tedious, but at least we could rest our eyes.

The long trips away from home and family often gave railroad crews a story or two to tell. Some guys said with a smile, "My own wife, kids, and even the dog don't know me." Sometimes, marriages and relationships ended in divorce or separation. Such stories never end. Every railroader has at least one.

My story involves a cat. During a slowdown, the railroad had furloughed me for a few months. It happens on every railroad. My neighbor, Deb, thought I seemed lonely and maybe needed a companion. Deb's cat, Country Boots, had a litter of kittens, and Deb brought a cute tabby tiger with gray and white stripes over for me to see and hold.

Deb also brought all the fixin's with her: litter, litter box, food. How could I resist? But, I thought, no way. I am gone sometimes two and three days at a time when I'm working road jobs.

Deb responded quickly and said, "Cats are fine. You can leave them with plenty of food and water, and they will eat and sleep, sleep and eat. You know, the tough life of a cat."

Deb's persistence won me over, and I became the proud owner of a kitten named Kittybell. She wore a white collar with a bell. She got used to her new home and her new two-legged mom. It wasn't long before she took over and ruled the entire home. By the time I was twenty-seven, I graduated from apartment living when I built my first home in Chesapeake City, Maryland.

My home became Kittybell's turf. Sometimes, I was gone on a long trip for three or, sometimes, four days. When I finally got home, I could see her waiting in the window. I put the key in the door and opened it, and that cat came running into the kitchen, stopped, sat there, and then looked at me as if to say, "Where the hell have you been?" Soon she warmed up to me, and all was well again.

Susie at home in Maryland with Kittybell

Other times, I worked a local job and finished in from eight to twelve hours. I arrived at home, put the key in the door, opened it, and Kitty only peeked around the corner into the kitchen, sat there, and stared at me as if to say, "What?? Home so soon?" Then she would walk away. Seemed I disturbed her quality quiet time. Go figure.

Pets make really good companions. Kittybell stayed with me for sixteen years, and she and I enjoyed life together.

As an engineer, I worked different class trains. They required the engineer to know how to handle each one with precision. There was little room for error, but we are human and can make mistakes, unfortunately not without consequences that sometimes result in extreme damage and fatality.

Anyone can learn to operate a locomotive and run it up and down a straight piece of track, but it takes the real skill of an engineer to couple several 3,000-, 4,000-, 5,000-, or 6,000-horsepower locomotives together and couple to a 7,000- to 17,000-ton train of from 80 to 125 cars, sit behind the controls, and move that train smoothly up and down steep grades, around curves, over trestles and river bridges, and through tunnels. Engineers have the skill to operate trains under cities, under water as when traveling through the East River or the Hudson into New York, or on the Baltimore and Potomac Railroad into Baltimore through interlockings, and in and out of huge railroad yards in all kinds of weather.

A railroad engineer takes sole responsibility for safe handling and control of a train at all times. There is little room for error. A railroad engineer must stay alert and fully focused, and nothing is more important than knowing where the train is at all times.

People often asked, "Susie, what is it like to run a train?"

My answer: "Exhilarating. A great, overwhelming feeling of pride, power, and responsibility.

"I sit in the seat behind the controls looking at a panel of gauges, air pressure, reservoir, brake pipe, rpms, speedometer, switches, and buttons. It is the engineer's control stand. I release the brakes and place my fingertips on the throttle of 3,000, 6,000, 9,000, or 12,000 horsepower pulling between 80 and 125 cars of incredible tonnage and cargo.

"I take a deep breath, my heart pounding, and I slowly begin to notch back the throttle one notch at a time. The big steel wheels start to turn, and the train begins to move. I hear the high-pitched sound of turbocharged engines pulling with all they've got. I feel the power and vibration through my body."

When the train accelerates to its normal, allowed track speed, the engine starts to rock slowly from side to side. This is an awesome feeling. For me, nothing in the world equaled it. So many have dreamed of the feeling, but very few experience it. When I felt it, it numbered among the proudest moments of my life. I felt privileged, and I will never forget those exhilarating moments of glory sometimes interrupted by unpredictable moments of sheer terror.

Here are just a few of my moments of unpredictable, sheer terror.

The Day the Airbrakes Failed

On a beautiful day in early September, 1981, I got myself up and ready to leave my home for work. I worked on an Amtrak passenger job out of Washington to New York City, Train 186. I drove my car to Wilmington Station to meet with my co-engineer, Danny Fisher. Together, we deadheaded on a train to DC to board our scheduled train to New York. Catching a ride on the train was much more convenient than driving the distance in your car, and it didn't cost us money.

Danny was my senior engineer and had many years behind the throttle of high-speed passenger trains, then rolling along over concrete ties and ribbons of welded rail at between 110 and 120 miles per hour. Danny and I worked the job together for several months at a time, and the trips always went smoothly with a pretty good on-time performance record. I learned a lot working with Danny as senior, and of course, we split running of the train at halfway points, either at Wilmington or Philadelphia

We arrived at Washington Union Station in plenty of time, got our orders from the office, and boarded the head end of our train, 186, Track 4. Our lead locomotive was a Class AEM7

Engineer Susie ready to board Amtrak Class E 60 954 locomotive at the Ivy City engine pit in Washington, DC

electric engine of 7,000 horsepower pulling seven Amfleet Pullman cars. The crew and we completed inspections and performed the mandatory airbrake test. All signals cleared to go.

Danny released the brakes, notched back the throttle, and the train made its way slowly out of the terminal through interlocking crossovers and out to the main line where normal speed could accelerate to 110 mph.

Our first scheduled stop was Baltimore, but not before dipping down underground through the B&P Tunnel.

Entering the tunnel required the engineer to apply some airbrake to slow the train then proceed through the tunnel and out the mouth to stop alongside the station platform in Baltimore. All brake systems worked fine, and we had no indication of any problems.

After all passengers departed and boarded, we got the all clear to go. We proceeded slowly out of Baltimore station to the main line and once again accelerated the train to track speed of 110 mph.

The next stop was Aberdeen Station, Maryland, a smaller, out-in-the-open station. The stop required the engineer to choose a landmark to apply some airbrake to slow the train speed while preparing to come to a smooth stop while lining up the train with the station platform.

When Danny approached his set landmark, he applied the airbrake to begin slowing the train. Neither of us felt the usual slight nudge or resistance experienced when applying the airbrake to a high-speed train. That feeling along with the instrument panel of gauges assures the engineer that brakes work and will slow the train.

Danny immediately applied more airbrake and instantly realized something was wrong. The train kept moving at 110 mph when it should have stopped at Aberdeen Station.

The airbrakes on the train were not working. We only had one single engine brake to slow the runaway train. The engine brakes and journals heated up fast, and sparks shot out from the wheels. In the dusk of early evening, it looked like Fourth of July fireworks.

a train about to cross the Susquehanna River Bridge along the
Amtrak Northeast Corridor at Havre de Grace, Maryland

As a young engineer, I honestly admit I was terrified. We could not slow or stop that train in enough time for the next interlocking crossover at Havre de Grace, Maryland, before crossing over the Susquehanna River bridge, a long bridge where no engineer wanted to stop a train for any reason. In daylight, I have looked out the locomotive window straight down into the water. Exhilarating and somewhat frightening. For me, getting across that bridge quickly gave me a sigh of relief each time throughout my railroad profession.

Although I was scared during the incident between Baltimore and Aberdeen stations, Danny remained calm and handled the situation with precision, better than anything I had ever seen in my time on the railroad.

He immediately called the forward tower operator and explained our situation. The tower operator quickly responded, said the railroad was lined and locked, and we had a clear block.

That definitely counted in our favor, but I thought I was going to die that night.

Danny shouted to me to brace myself because the train would hit the crossover hard. All I could think of was "We're going to jump the track and drop off into the river!" It is sometimes hard to think positive during such terrifying moments.

We hit the crossover very hard with an incredible jolt but stayed on the track and trudged across the deep, dark, scary Susquehanna River with the train slowing down some from losing momentum at the crossover and application of the single brake. It finally came to rest after the entire train cleared the river.

I could have kissed the ground. And, oh, yeah. Danny, too.

Amtrak Engineer Danny Fisher, one of
Susie's mentors in high speed passenger service

The conductor departed the train and walked forward to the engine to investigate. Usually, we communicated from between the engine and train by a telephone receiver on the locomotive, but as sometimes happened, it failed to work. In our case, it meant a big deal, because the usual, simple line of communication could have stopped the train immediately with the conductor pulling the emergency stop valve. If we had been able to ask for that, the emergency valve would automatically have applied all the air to the braking system through the entire train and quickly stopped it.

We did not know what caused the sudden loss of airbrake from the engine to the train or why the brakes failed.

We waited for a replacement engine out of Wilmington. The engine and train inspectors arrived and changed out the engine, and made a complete inspection of the train, airbrakes, and communication systems. The tower gave us authority to proceed.

The passengers in such a case don't normally know details of a delay nor what happened. The strategy assumes that if they know little or nothing, they will remain calm.

It was a hair-raising night for Danny and me. We looked at each other and sighed a big sigh of relief, although with a bewildered, unsettling feeling about what caused the brakes to fail. We wanted answers.

We arrived in New York late, climbed down off the train, and headed into the terminal to the office.

Danny was determined to inquire as to what happened to the equipment that night and why it failed. After some time passed without results, Danny persisted in pushing for answers. Our bosses told him a defective angle cock between the locomotive and first coach somehow worked itself closed through vibration and cut off the air supply to the train's brakes.

The answer did not entirely convince Danny, and the incident remained a hush, hush. You didn't read about it nor hear about it. I believe that night, some two hundred people rode that train. No one knew about it then and never will. Danny, however, always wondered about the way authorities handled that incident. He didn't like it, but eventually he stopped asking.

Several years passed, and Engineer Danny retired after close to forty years of railroading. He moved to Florida, but he kept in touch with me. In every letter he wrote, he said,

> *Susie,*
> *I will never forget the night we lost our airbrakes on*
> *Train 186.*
> *Keep rolling, and stay safe.*
> > *Danny*

The Man on the Track

One pleasant early summer evening. I worked an Amtrak job out of Washington to New York with a senior engineer, JP. Our train departed Washington Union Station, and we maintained an on-time schedule to Philadelphia.

We departed Philadelphia station on time, and the warm darkness of night had fallen around us. The locomotive headlight shone bright down the track ahead of us, the rails glistening. We accelerated the train to eighty miles per hour north of Philadelphia.

Suddenly we saw movement on the track ahead. At first, we thought we saw a deer or other animal we sometimes encountered en route. At 80 mph, the intensely bright locomotive headlight made things appear to approach fast in the night. When we both realized a human being stood in front of us on the track, JP immediately pulled the automatic brake handle over to emergency braking, better known in railroad terms as "dumping the air."

You cannot stop a passenger train doing eighty on a dime. We both stood up out of our seats, JP laying on the horn. We yelled out, kind of like cheering, "Get off. Jump, man, jump," but he stood looking straight ahead at us.

The train struck him at 69 mph as it began to slow down but not quickly enough to save the man on the tracks.

An awful sound like a thud and slight wheel slip left a terrible feeling inside of me. We knew a precious life had ended quickly with nothing we could do.

The train came to rest and authorities notified. The conductor got off the train and walked forward to the engine to inquire why we had stopped.

We continued to New York after authorities inspected the scene and located the body. I had an unsettled feeling in my gut that would remain in memory for some time. I had never witnessed a suicide. It left me shaken and quiet.

I will never forget the man dressed in a white tee shirt and white jeans. He stood out on the tracks like the moon on a clear summer night against a black sky and stared us down to end his life.

He succeeded.

The Car that Hit the Train

On a late fall afternoon as the sun began to set slowly, I worked a freight train out of Harrington, Delaware, to Harrisburg, Pennsylvania. The train consisted of two 3,800-horsepower SD60 engines in the lead and a hundred cars behind me.

The train ran along on the Delmarva secondary track at forty miles per hour, a pretty good moving freight through flat, open fields with visibility for miles.

I approached my next road crossing set at a slight angle and intended for autos. The setting sun and angle can blind a driver.

As I began to sound the whistle on the approach to the crossing, I could see a car nearing the gates. It did not slow down, and suddenly, the car slammed into the fuel tank of my second engine. I caught it out of my peripheral vision and could see the hood of the car airborne and the car itself wrapped around the crossing gate.

The train had moved into a curve, and I lost sight of the auto while waiting for my train to stop completely after I activated emergency braking. My conductor, train dispatcher, and I

Engine 6104 en route from Harrington, Delaware, to Harrisburg, Pennsylvania

communicated immediately in accordance with procedure that indicates authorities will then arrive at the accident scene. The conductor always walks along the train after an accident and talks to authorities. As the engineer, I remained on the engine in contact with the train dispatcher and conductor.

After some time passed, the conductor returned to the engine and confirmed that the car had struck the second engine's fuel tank with minor damage. I would officially report the damage when I completed the run. The accident totaled the car. Emergency personnel pulled the young woman driver and her three small children from the wreckage and transported them to the hospital.

My conductor said it didn't look good. As an engineer, I can say that sometimes you just don't want to know the outcome because you don't want it to haunt you or make you feel you could have done something to prevent an accident.

In the aftermath of the accident, we got authority to proceed, because we had a long way to go to get to our destination in Harrisburg. On we went. A sick feeling remained inside me. I was quiet for the entire trip.

It just affects you that way, and you never really forget it.

The Race to the Crossing

A fresh blanket of snow had fallen in mid December. I got called out to take a hopper train or empty coal train from the Delmarva Power Plant in Delaware to Harrisburg. The Indian River secondary track speed was thirty miles per hour, a pretty good speed for moving freight. I had two 3,000-horsepower SD40-2 engines in the lead with a hundred empty hopper cars behind me.

The local road ran parallel to the railroad track for miles, and I often saw autos alongside wanting to race or just pace along as they kept up with the train. Some drivers were just fun-loving rail fans.

On that beautiful early evening, light snow began to softly fall from the sky and landed on the engine's windshield. I noticed a small black pickup truck pacing alongside me. It continued for miles. I could see a fresh-cut Christmas tree in the truck bed. It was that time of year again, everyone picking up Christmas trees and holiday shopping. It was a peaceful, cozy, joyful time of year.

As I approached one of many road crossings, I lost sight of the truck behind some of the town's buildings. I could clearly see my

a fresh blanket of snow in December, 1986

crossing gates down and flashing. As I blew the whistle for the crossing, the pickup truck came suddenly around the gate onto the track.

I stood up out of my seat, and in seconds, the locomotive struck the pickup truck between the cab and truck bed, pushing it down the track and off to the side.

Emergency braking slowed the train, and finally it came to rest. By then, the damaged pickup sat disabled somewhere behind us. It never dawned on me when I lost sight of the pickup behind the buildings that the driver would try to beat me to the next crossing.

As I suddenly saw the truck and stood up out of my seat, my sight fell right on the young man driving just split seconds before impact. I saw the same young man who earlier waved to me as he paced the train. I saw the terrified look on a human face staring at a huge locomotive coming straight at him.

That look froze in time and my memory.

I will never forget that image.

Never.

Did he make it? I will only tell you that I had enough of that image. I did not need to know more.

Tanker at the Crossing

On another beautiful sunshiny afternoon, I got the call to take a loaded coal train from Harrington, Delaware, down to Delmarva Power Plant. Three SD40-2 engines in the lead at 9,000 horsepower and 17 thousand tons of coal. A very heavy train, indeed.

Proceeding out of Harrington, train speed is ten miles per hour. It takes some time for a train to clear the yard before it can begin to accelerate to the thirty mile-per-hour track speed.

Continuing along at 10 mph, the train approaches a very busy road crossing. A signal system protects it, but at rush hour, it doesn't matter. Nobody wants to stop and wait for a freight train going at 10 mph. At rush hour, traffic tends to back up at the traffic signal ahead. Cars and trucks can freely move along even though the overhead warning lights flash. And then, the vehicles get backed up at the traffic light.

The process of clearing the yard takes time, and as the train nears the multiple crossing, the engineer lays on the whistle and doesn't let up. At a distance, cars and trucks whiz across the railroad tracks at the crossing.

I didn't start to get nervous until I saw traffic backing up and stopping. As engineer, I saw a horrific sight in front of me that day. A Texaco tanker truck pinned between stopped traffic sat dead center across the tracks.

I had to make a decision. The last thing an engineer wants to hit with a train is a tanker truck. Imagine the explosion! I had heard actual stories about such events when engine crews burned to death.

Well, my heart dropped into my feet, and I made the decision to put the train into emergency braking. Even a train going only 10 mph with that kind of tonnage cannot stop on a dime. The train stopped, but it was close. Too close.

I don't think the driver of the tanker even knew. Really, people just want to get to their destinations, whatever it takes.

That one took my breath away.

A Moment of Paranoia

One very foggy evening, I was called to take a train out of Harrington, Delaware, to Harrisburg, Pennsylvania.

The Delmarva Branch, a secondary track, uses a manual block signal system, which requires authority to the engineer from the train dispatcher in Philadelphia before a train can proceed. The route crossed over the Chesapeake and Delaware Canal, called the C and D Canal, a busy waterway for large ships, tugboats, and smaller vessels.

The bridge across the canal remains in the up position unless lowered by a local bridge tender when a train crosses over. The bridge consists of a single track and manual block signal governing a train over the bridge.

Passing over the canal in daylight hours never bothered me, because I could see the bridge in the down position with track lined up straight ahead, but in the darkest of night, I had a totally different feeling. Yes, indeed.

A signal governs the train, and clear verbal communication between the bridge tender and engineer is crucial.

On that particular dark, dense, foggy night, I became disoriented. Somehow, in that moment of paranoia, I lost faith in the bridge tender who had just told me that the bridge was down, lined, and locked. He said, "Bring it on."

As I notched out on the throttle, I could feel the train moving, but I could not see anything ahead of me in the dense fog. I could not see my headlight shining on the rail ahead as I could on a clear night. I could not tell where the bridge was.

My mind turned like fast-moving hands on a clock. I felt so uneasy. I kept thinking, "The bridge is not down." I felt I would run out of track and the locomotives would suddenly plunge to the bottom of the cold, deep, dark canal waters and I would be trapped and drown.

I could actually feel that terrifying sensation chilling my entire body like it would actually happen.

It felt so real, so frightening, and so creepy. It took me a while to re-collect my thoughts and get focused to complete the trip.

My moment of paranoia provides a good example of what engineers deal with in adverse weather conditions. I had heard and read about similar incidents when such tragedies actually occurred.

I experienced many moments of fright during my railroad career. I do not miss them.

Several more years passed, and the life of a railroad engineer began to take its toll on me. I grew tired and weary of long hours away from home day after day. My packed bags always waited by the door.

Whenever I lay my tired body down and my head came to rest on the pillow, I fell right to sleep until the kitchen telephone awakened me. The kitchen was the ideal place for the telephone, because I needed physically to get up out of bed to answer it.

Sometimes, I lay my head down at 11 PM and got awakened by a call from the crew dispatcher at 1, 2, or 3 AM. When I heard the phone ring, I often put the pillow over my head and whined, "No! No!"

That's the life of a railroad engineer. It really takes great self-discipline to keep up that kind of pace, and I must say, I kept up with the best of them. Yes, I did.

The road jobs I liked. I was single and didn't mind being gone two or three days at a time. It was the local yard jobs I didn't care for: making up trains with a lot of back and forth switching. I never felt comfortable having to turn my head continuously in different directions, resulting in a stiff neck.

Constant repetitious motion became tedious. Perhaps my small stature and the way I had to position myself in the seat to see out the window and reach the controls contributed to my discomfort. Yard and local jobs bored me. I wanted to run the freights over the main line in one direction only: straight ahead. I was born to be an over-the-road freight engineer. That's where my heart was.

After almost thirteen years of continuous railroading working an extra board, I once again grew weary.

One morning, I got called out in mid July with ninety-five-degree, hot, humid weather to work a local shifter, one of those jobs I didn't especially like. Locomotives had no AC back in the day. You just did the best you could to endure.

The job consisted of making up a train. The task takes time and a lot of shifting and moving from track to track around the yard and in and out of local mills along a secondary track. As the hours carried on, I felt like the damned job would never end. I felt extremely hot, frustrated, irritable, uncomfortable, and tired. My clothes soaked in sweat. When your pants and underwear are wet, you become so, so uncomfortable.

At close to twelve hours of continuous shifting and moving around, I had had just about enough. Remember, the law says an engineer can operate a train for not more than twelve hours on a single shift. And then, often, more hours accumulated while I waited for pick-up by a local cab company or railroad van to get back to the yard office. Sometimes I got left in out-of-the-way places, and I waited a while. Sometimes the job ended up a fourteen- to sixteen-hour day.

The train dispatcher in Philadelphia who gave me authority to operate over the railroad throughout the day knew me well. He knew my voice, and that day, he detected something different.

I did not know at the time, but the train dispatcher Williams thought he had detected early signs of a possible breakdown. He recognized it because he himself had gone through something similar on his job when the railroad assigned him more and more responsibility. He heard me say over the airway for anyone to hear, "I cannot take one more minute on this locomotive." Then I choked up. I said, "I want to get the hell off this engine right now."

My conductor kept telling me, "Hang in there, Susie. We're almost done." Well, many more hours later, I finally made it home and crashed on the couch.

Later that day, I got a phone call from Train Dispatcher Williams, who was very concerned about me and wanted to make sure I was okay. Now, train dispatchers don't ever call you. Only crew dispatchers call you. Train dispatchers control the authority for trains to use certain tracks. Crew dispatchers call the crews for each job.

It surprised me to get that call from Williams, and we talked a while. Because he felt I was on the verge of having a nervous breakdown, he wanted to help me, starting by just talking.

I'm glad he did, because I did need help. I was nearing the end of my rope. All the years of all I had taken on that job finally caught up with me. I could feel it in my mind and body. I was beginning to break.

Now, granted, I was as tough as the toughest, but there comes a time when toughness gets tried over and over again. A person then needs to recognize the breaking point and stop it before it is too late. Thanks to one kind-hearted train dispatcher, I got that chance to catch myself before falling too far. A few out there really understood and cared, even though most of the time, I was on my own.

I took some time off. I got the help I needed and plenty of good rest. I went back home to Buffalo to see the family. I needed that. I lived in Chesapeake City, Maryland, so I had about a seven-hour drive to Buffalo.

After about a month of leave, I returned to work and felt good again on the trains. I worked steady for several more years. The railroad business prospered, and work was plentiful.

A few more years of non-stop railroading went by, and once again, I got tired in more ways than one.

One day in the yard, I saw white smoke coming from the engine cab of a standing locomotive. I climbed aboard and immediately shut the engine down but not before inhaling a good dose of white smoke from the electrical cabinet. It made me feel faint, so I ended up in the local emergency room for some oxygen until they released me.

Railroad officials thanked me and recognized me for my quick thinking. I saved a locomotive from further damage, and it didn't go unnoticed.

In spite of such rewarding moments, the railroad had become my whole life, a rather lonely life. I made good money, yes, but money cannot take the place of health, and my health felt like it was taking a dive to the bottom. Anxiety, stress levels, and long hours began to weaken me mentally, emotionally, and physically.

Many railroaders experienced the ever-present high-risk factor of burnout. More and more human error occurred because of fatigue from overwork and overwhelming demands in all fields of the railroad. More wrecks, injuries, and loss of life. I did not want to miss out on living. I was still young. I loved the railroad, being an engineer, and running the trains, but I didn't want it to run me into an early grave. I had to make a decision about my life and well-being.

The Ignorance of Harassment

At twenty-five years old in 1978, I entered the man's world of railroading. Growing up, I had heard the word harassment, and I understood it to mean annoy, disturb, tease, or taunt persistently.

I kind of knew before I ever started the railroad job that it could be tough and perhaps some men would get their kicks by harassing and teasing me. The new world I entered had seemed more glamorous than it turned out.

I have to say that, for the most part, the men showed acceptance and respect. However, a minority did not.

Things in the work force slowly began to change in the late 1970s, and more women with spunk and grit stepped up to the plate to give these types of jobs their best shot. I numbered among those women.

I am a person who always felt an inner toughness, an iron will spirit. I had dogged determination. I would not give up or back down without a good fight. Probably I inherited incredible spirit from my beloved mother and her Scottish heritage.

The railroad yard offices, break rooms, locker rooms, and bathrooms often were pretty disgusting. Pornographic magazines

Susie, the engineer in control of a
6,000-horsepower Class E60 Amtrak train,
Night Owl, *from Washington, DC, to New York City*

piled on tables for the guys. Nude pin-up posters of young female models hung on the walls everywhere. I could not avoid seeing them, and, yes, I must say it was pretty embarrassing.

In those days, almost everyone smoked something. Ashtrays overflowed and smelled awful. Cigarette butts, cigar butts, and pipe ashes littered the floors, grounds, and locomotive cabs. To me, it was not a pretty world. But, hey. I had a job in a man's world of railroading, and I felt I just had to put on my big girl pants, tighten my belt, be firm, and just take it. And take it, I did.

I also saw dangerous drug and alcohol abuse. I remember working in the yard at night with a senior engineer when the conductor, known to carry a fifth of whiskey in his pocket, fell over at the switch. My engineer and brakeman helped him up. At my young age, I didn't really know what to think about it.

Times were changing, but they weren't changing quite enough. Like every young female, I had a monthly menstrual cycle. Under the conditions and bathroom availability, that was very tough to handle, especially during twelve-hour days on an engine. Let me just say that I managed and leave it at that.

In the early 1980s, you could slowly see change. The railroad built yard offices and renovated old ones with cleaner restrooms for men and women. Very few nude magazines sat on tables, and few nude pinups hung on the walls. That good start made the environment of my job more presentable. Let's keep in mind that I did not ask for the changes nor complain about previous conditions. I came as I was and dealt with everything around me as it was, the man's world of railroading that I alone did not intend to change.

As I fell deeper into that man's world, I always felt the need to respect and be respected by my coworkers in all fields. I made sure I looked the part. I dressed appropriately—the usual blue jeans, tee shirts, vest, boots, and ball cap. Some of the men said, "She's as cute as a bug's ear." I didn't mind that, not at all.

Sometimes, the men asked questions about my life: Are you married? Do you have any kids? Someone once asked if I were a lesbian. I always answered their questions honestly. The questions did not offend me.

Most guys were nice. However, a few tried to get more than small talk and simple answers.

I lived in an apartment complex, and I went home after working a twelve-hour night shift. When I got out of my car, one morning, a middle-aged engineer named Tommy met me. He waited for me in the parking lot. He knew my work schedule.

I was surprised to see him. I had met him at the yard a few times. I asked him if he lived in the same complex.

He said, "No." I realized why he waited for me. He wanted me to invite him in for breakfast and coffee. Yeah, right!! I remained calm and smiled. I stood my ground and firmly said, "No."

I had encountered similar acts by men at other times in other places, and I continued to stand my ground.

Why didn't I report such incidents to the authorities? The answer is, I worked in this man's world doing a man's job. There were a lot more of them than me, and when I thought about reporting an offensive moment, I asked myself, "Who will my superiors believe? Them or me?" I had put too much of my life into that incredible dream and accomplishment. I did not want to cause any trouble, especially for myself.

Sometimes, some guy gave me the ol' shoulder rub to see how I would respond to being touched and how far I might go. I've got to admit, in fact, that sometimes, it felt soooooo good I just wanted to melt with every touch.

Now, look. I may have been petite and cute, but I was no centerfold beauty queen. I thought at times those poor guys were just desperate for affection. Through the years, I continuously dealt with it. I always stood my ground regardless of my own potential weakness.

Now, let me tell you the story of a little engineer named Glenn. He worked the extra board for Amtrak. He caught a job with me during the absence of my regular assigned engineer, who was on vacation. Glenn was about forty and not especially attractive, at least not to me.

We worked the Train 188 to New York from Washington. Glenn somehow got a notion that when we took rest in New York, we would share a hotel room. At first, I thought he was kidding, but he kept bringing it up during the whole 226-mile trip. I just found him obnoxious and ignored him.

When we arrived at New York's Penn Station and were ready to climb down off the engine, Glenn took hold of my arm. I turned, and he pulled me into him and started to kiss me, saying, "You're going to the hotel with me, aren't you?"

Let me just say that I disappointed ole Glenn, who portrayed a severely bruised ego.

Awwwwwww. Poor Glenn.

On the return trip to Washington, Glenn did not speak to me for the entire 226 miles. Frankly, I didn't give a damn.

What follows tops it all, and I will explain it to the best of my ability and memory.

It begins when I took a regular job with Amtrak called the *Night Owl*, Train 178-67 at that time, departing Washington at 3:20 PM and arriving in New York Penn Station at 8:25 PM.

I had been working steady with a regular senior engineer named Tom. Tom went on vacation, and the engineers' extra board then filled the job.

A couple of trips along, I drew a senior engineer named CD. I did not know CD. I had never before met him. He was in his late sixties and close to retiring. I learned he had a good reputation for running a train with almost forty years' experience.

He was a father type. I liked him. He did not smoke, drink, chew snuff, or spit in a cup. He carried a bible. I thought, "Oh, my. What a refreshing change." He was a family man, married with children and grandchildren.

I enjoyed working with him during the first two trips we made, and after a trip off, I went to work and caught up with CD again for the third time. Seems he caught the job regularly. It just works like that sometimes. Nothing unusual. I was glad to see him.

We left Washington on time, heading to New York. Most engineers split running the train at halfway points like Wilmington or Philadelphia. On the return trip, I got the unexpected shock of my life.

All had gone smoothly on our return trip. At Wilmington Station, CD turned the train over to me to complete the trip. We departed Wilmington on time, heading south to Washington. Our speed for this train was 80 mph, the restricted speed of the Class E60 locomotive built by General Electric. I felt good on that sunshine-filled morning. We maintained an on-time schedule. As we rolled along, CD got up and went through the door directly behind the engineer's seat into the engine room compartment that houses the toilet.

I gave it no thought. Engineers went there all the time.

At 80 mph, we approached Iron Hill, a rather steep grade located in Maryland that required the engineer to apply a little airbrake before the long descent. I focused totally on my location as I sought my landmark to apply the airbrake. I heard the compartment door behind me open and slam shut as CD re-entered the cab.

I felt his presence behind me and gave it no thought. I remained straight ahead focused and in full control of the train. Suddenly, I felt CD take my hand off the automatic brake handle and place it on his exposed, erect penis. His open pants hung halfway down.

*Susie engineering for Amtrak on 178 in
Washington in 1981*

It all happened so suddenly and unexpectedly. I quickly took my hand back, but that split-second distraction caused me to miss my landmark to apply the train's airbrake, and the train accelerated down the grade at ninety miles per hour. The train's over-speed and alert alarms kept sounding, and the train went into automatic stop.

However, I acted fast enough to pull the automatic airbrake handle to the suppression position which, if done fast enough, allows the engineer to suppress the automatic train stop penalty and prevent the train from stopping completely. I succeeded and managed to kick off the brake and keep the train in a slow rolling motion until I could get air pressure up and the train back to normal speed.

I gave myself an A+ performance on that one for quick reaction time. Amen!

Once I regained full control and got the train back to speed, I looked over at CD and yelled at him, "What were you thinking? Why did you do that?"

I then noticed he had ejaculated on the engine compartment floor behind me. I threw a bottle of water and handful of paper towels at him and said, "Clean it up."

I told him I planned to report this insane incident to the railroad foreman in DC. I was furious and shaking, because I knew I had done nothing to provoke such unacceptable behavior.

Realizing what he had done and the possible consequences of his action, CD apologized and pleaded with me to forgive him and not report it.

I did not speak for the remainder of the trip. He remained completely quiet. He really disappointed me, because I previously had a great respect for him.

I asked myself, "What made him do this?" He was so close to retirement.

I would never know the answer nor would the authorities nor the 270 passengers on the train that morning.

Once again, here is a good example of my approach to harassment. There are more of them and only one of me. Who would they believe? Where could reporting something like that have left me?

I told myself what they don't know won't hurt them and won't hurt me. I said to myself, "CD, you won this one this time." Hopefully, his maker forgave him and he now rests in peace.

As for me, I will never forget that day, and I am glad I finally did tell someone that crazy incident really happened. Some years later, after CD retired, I caught up with my now-retired union rep. He was shocked. He told me I should have reported the incident immediately. He said, no, I did not have to take that. That's how I learned about the real meaning of sexual harassment and what it is all about. Better known as "Live and learn."

I have many more similar stories, I wanted to give you one good, clear example of what I encountered as a young female railroad engineer.

Such incidents and behavior over the years took their toll on me mentally, emotionally, and physically. It badly beat me down. I felt hurt and embarrassed by both words and actions from certain men. I often broke down only when alone, because I didn't want to show any sign of weakness or defeat nor did I want to have to explain anything to anyone.

Engineer Susie finishing a work train on the
Amtrak Northeast Corridor in 1987

The Wreck of Amtrak's Colonial

My mind goes back some thirty years. I become nervous and anxious as I remember the breaking news about the Amtrak train, *The Colonial* passenger train out of Washington en route to New York City on the Northeast Corridor. I shake each time I'm confronted with what happened, on this occasion, not to me nor on a train I was operating at the time.

On January 4, 1987, at home, I tuned into breaking news about a train that crashed on the Northeast Corridor at Chase, Maryland. As an engineer, I knew the location well. I had run such high-speed trains up and down the corridor for years, and I had worked *The Colonial*.

wreck of Amtrak's Colonial *in 1987*

photo from Wikimedia Commons.com

The crash involved *The Colonial* and three coupled ConRail light engines out of Baltimore near Chase. I knew the engineer operating the ConRail locomotives. I worked with Ricky from time to time and had worked with him on the same light-engine job out of Baltimore to Harrisburg.

I always felt uncomfortable working with Ricky, as I had witnessed the use of illegal drugs on the job and on the engine. Both Ricky and the brakeman did not hide what they did. I recognized it as dangerous behavior, but I did *nothing!* Sometimes when you think you should report unusual behavior to authorities, you also think you don't need to make trouble for a co-worker and become known as untrustworthy among them.

We had taken some light engines to Harrisburg via the Port Road Brach. At the time, I worked the extra list and got called out on the job.

With Ricky, I felt unsettled in my mind and in my gut the whole trip. I did not like the feeling, and it continued to tug at me. I just wanted to get the job done, get back, go home, and forget about it. I thought if I should ever again get called out to work with him, I would just call out sick.

I never could predict a happening in the near future, but something was going on with me, and it wouldn't leave me alone. I kept thinking I was overtired. Soon the feeling subsided, and I was back on track.

I did not know then, but I later found that I suffered from chronic anxiety disorder. I had panic attacks from time to time. When panic attacks occurred, and they did at any time and anywhere, I thought I would die. I would describe it as feeling as if my blood boiled through my veins. My heart raced, and

wreck of Amtrak's **Colonial** *in 1987*

I'd be soaked in sweat, a frightening experience when you don't understand what is happening.

My panic attacks occurred more frequently, and the day I heard the news about the crash, I had one. During the attacks, a person becomes frightened, thus manifesting more fear. You try to run away from yourself. I always tried to find a bathroom to splash cold water on my face and sit down. The feeling leaves as quickly as it comes, but it leaves a person jittery and weak for a short time.

As more footage and aerial views came on the news, I learned that *The Colonial* had two Class AEM7s in the lead when it hit three linked ConRail locomotives that ran a stop signal and proceeded out to the main line in the same block as *The Colonial* passenger train. On impact at 120 mph, the lead engine exploded, instantly killing the engineer. The Amfleet passenger cars behind the engines folded like an accordion and jumped the track. What a horrific sight. Heart-wrenching!

After the investigation, I got an extra board call out on a work train to go to the location of the crash and start hauling and cleaning up the equipment involved. We had to bring the wreckage to a specific location in the yard.

I felt so nervous and anxious when I got called for that job. I had an empty, sick feeling. It was the worst job I ever had to work. I thought that the accident could have happened to me, as I had worked *The Colonial* for countless trips. It felt like a horror movie when you actually could hear the ghostly screams and cries of those who lived and died in that wreckage.

I choked on my tears, which seemed to run down the back of my throat as I slowly ran my engine by the wreckage. Somewhere deep down inside, I felt like maybe it was time to find a new career. I was still young. I wanted to live a life with less stress and risk.

I could hardly imagine doing anything else but running trains for the railroad.

The railroad was my heart and soul of an American Dream. It meant everything I had accomplished in my young life. How could I walk away?

A tragedy like the wreck of *The Colonial* doesn't just go away. It stays and, from time to time, you relive a piece of that memory. For me, it has been some thirty years, and I still ask myself, Was there something I should have done possibly to prevent a tragedy like that from happening? I feel I should have reported the use of illegal drugs on the job and on the trains.

If I had done my part and reported what I had witnessed, then perhaps Ricky and his brakeman would have been questioned, drug-tested, and pulled out of service. It then would have taken some time to fight everything with the union and be returned to service. I still ask myself if I had done the right thing and reported the crew using drugs, perhaps a more competent and focused ConRail crew would have been on that light-engine job out of Baltimore on January 4, 1987. Then, perhaps that horrifying, senseless tragedy would not have happened.

I know now, after thirty years, how important it is for all of us to do our part and report unusual or unlawful behavior in the workplace. It just might save a precious life. I knew Jerome Evans, the Amtrak engineer whose life ended in seconds that day. My heartfelt thoughts and sincere condolences go out to all who suffered loss and injury on the Amtrak Colonial that day.

My Opinion

I did not agree with Amtrak's decision to take one person off the engine, thus leaving one engineer to operate high speed trains alone. An engineer is a human being, and human beings make mistakes. Engineers (and all people) can not perform 24/7, perfect all the time nor can they depend totally on failsafe systems.

I always believed in safety first. Safety should always be the first priority, especially when an engineer works in passenger train service, transporting precious lives every day.

If an engineer for any reason misses something or becomes suddenly incapacitated due to a health issue, a second engineer on that engine can respond immediately, as trained.

Amtrak made the decision to cut crew size. Time and time again since, the policy has proven not to be failsafe. Trains crash, and we hear about them in breaking news or read about them in newspapers.

I realize that railroading is big business and must do what must be done to survive, but I don't agree that the measures should take place at the expense of common sense and safety.

No corporation should sacrifice safety for financial survival or gain. Eventually, something will happen, possibly with fatal results.

The End of a Dream • Susie's Farewell

My packed bags waited by the door.

I got called out of Harrington, Delaware, to take an empty coal hopper train to Enola Yard in Pennsylvania.

It was just another day on the railroad. I had my favorite crew accompanying me, and I had three of my favorite Class SD40-2 locomotives with 9,000 horsepower and a hundred empty hoppers. I couldn't have planned a better set-up. I felt good, and everything went smoothly.

We had a pleasant and safe trip to our destination. I had a fine meal and plenty of good sleep at the hotel.

After ten hours, we got called for our return trip out of Enola Yard. The cab picked us up and took us to the yard office, where we got our orders. I got my three favorite engines back to take us home to Harrington, this time with a hundred cars loaded with coal.

This is what I called a sweet train. I loved coal trains, especially with three 3,000-horsepower SD40-2 engines.

We climbed aboard, made our brake test, and got permission to depart the yard and proceed out to the main line, where we

Susie ready to serve as engineer on her favorite 3,000-horsepower EMD SD40-2 locomotive at Harrington Yard, Delaware

could accelerate the train to fifty miles per hour. I loved pulling the heavy coal trains in the eighth notch, the whining sound of the turbocharged diesel engines screaming and pulling hard. To me, this was top-notch railroading at its best.

We departed Harrisburg late in the evening, and as with most freights, we crept through the night and had to stop at different locations for passing trains on the Port Road Branch.

About this point, you begin to get a little tired and want to close your eyes while waiting for the train dispatcher or signal to give you authority to proceed. Hey. We all caught a wink or two when we could. It just happens. We worked long-hour mileage jobs, and running a freight train for twelve hours was tough.

I have taken in many sunsets and sunrises from the cab window of a locomotive. Always an awesome sight. As we sat on the train, I could see the full moon glistening on rippling river water. A peaceful feeling consumed me. We were stopped, and we were safe. That is always a good feeling, but I knew we still had a long way to go to get to our home destination.

After about forty minutes, we got a clear signal to proceed. I switched on the headlight to bright and released the brakes, my hand on the throttle pulling it back one notch at a time. The turbocharged diesel engines—with a total of nine-thousand horsepower—revved up together, and the steel wheels started to turn slowly.

Engineers can tell when they have all the train stretched together. My first senior engineer, JW, taught me that many years before, running a train by the seat of your pants. It's true. You can feel your train and what it is doing from the seat. At least, I could.

As we rounded our first of many curves along the Susquehanna River, I saw in the distance the headlight of the train we had been waiting on. He should have been in the siding, but something didn't look right, because his headlight still shone bright, making it very difficult to see just exactly where he was.

I stood up and asked my conductor, who was also standing, "He is in the siding, isn't he?"

I cannot really explain that feeling of momentary doubt, but I can tell you it takes your breath away when you see a train coming in your direction in the darkest of night with a headlight blinding you. You hold your breath until you either pass the train or collide.

In this case, he sat in the siding with his headlight still on bright. We gave a long sigh of relief and began breathing again. Whew!

*inside the cab of an EMD SD40-2 3,000-horsepower locomotive
like the one Susie operated on her final run*

Normally, I would have had confidence in the safe operations of the railroad on everyone's account, but because of memories of past incidents of human error, irresponsibility, injury, and loss of life, my complete trust that everything is okay had somewhat diminished over the years. I took nothing for granted.

It is hard to believe what we got away with from 1978 to 1987, when I was an engineer. Some guys taped over or cut out audible alert systems or clamped down the dead-man pedal, the pedal the engineer had to hold down by foot for the duration of a trip. It was the automatic train control: you take your foot off the pedal, an audible whistle sounds, and after about six seconds, air for the brakes begins automatically applying to stop the train.

We did not want that to happen nor did we want to sit there for hours in one position with a foot on the pedal. Sometimes, engineers used the red twenty-four-inch utility flag stick to hold down a deadman pedal. They jammed the stick between the pedal and up under the console. It worked nicely.

I will not admit to defeating train safety or monitoring systems on my train, but I will admit to witnessing them and saying nothing. Yes, you can say this is just as bad, and I will agree.

At the time, I thought, "Who am I to question the operations of my senior engineers?" They had been around the railroad a lot longer than I had. I trusted those men and that they knew what they were doing. Who was I to question old-time work habits? Here again, it was still a man's world of railroading, and who was I to change it?

I wanted to be liked, not despised. No way did I ever want to become known as Little Miss Tattletale. I learned the real meaning of being between a rock and a hard place.

On that beautiful night in Pennsylvania, our train maintained a nice, steady speed of thirty miles per hour. As it snaked its way around the mountain along the river, dawn began to break. Another morning sunrise on the railroad. Another awesome sight.

We approached the Amtrak main line at Perryville Interlocking. The tower operator always did his best to get us out on the main line and out of the way of passenger trains to avoid delays.

It was the high-speed Northeast Corridor. You could run your freight train at fifty miles per hour, getting it over the steep grades. Running trains with that kind of power, tonnage, and speed over concrete ties and ribbons of welded rail made for total railroading at its best. Nothing felt the same.

Davis Tower on the Amtrak Northeast Corridor

On the approach to Davis Interlocking, the tower operator Robinson—Robby—always said, "Hello, Susie," and put us on the Delmarva secondary track. We then got further authority from the train dispatcher out of Philadelphia to operate over the Delmarva secondary track and head for home.

The railroad ran at forty miles per hour over mainly flat land and open fields with a multitude of railroad crossings to blow the whistle for and wake up the towns. I loved that! I really did!

Our time grew short and close to our twelve-hour limit when we arrived outside the

Kendall "Robby" Robinson waiting to operate interlocking mechanisms at Davis Tower

Harrington Yard and likely to leave the train for another crew to finish up and take it to the Delmarva Power Plant.

Our time expired, and our trip ended outside the Harrington Yard office. We had completed another successful run. We were safe, and we were going home.

As I set the brakes on the train and engine and flipped all the necessary switches, I sat for a moment. An unsettled feeling came over me. I placed my hands on the controls, then rubbed my hands lightly over the console, and said aloud to myself, "Wow. Did I really do this American Railroad Dream? Yes. Yes, I did."

Engineer Susie ending a successful run from Harrisburg home to Harrington Yard

I got up out of the engineer's seat, grabbed my bag, and climbed down from the engine.

I did not plan what happened next, nor did I know I would do it. As I walked away from the train, I suddenly stopped, turned around, and put my bag down. I choked up and held back tears.

With my right hand, I saluted the three SD40-2 locomotives and said, "It was a successful run. Thank you for bringing me home safe once again.

"Farewell. I will miss you."

I wiped my face dry, picked up my bag, and walked across a few tracks to the yard office.

I went home, took a leave of absence, and never returned.

I didn't quit. I didn't resign. I wasn't fired. I simply walked away and never returned.

It was the hardest thing I ever did.

After all that I had dreamed of and all that I had accomplished—everything I experienced over fifteen years—I could honestly say, "It was one hell of an adventurous railroad career and a mighty fine picture-perfect, final run."

And to that, I say, Amen!

Rail Rider

by Bonnie Gaglia

to Susie Gaglia, my sister, the locomotive engineer

For fifteen years you have been riding the rails.
ConRail can be proud of you.
Our family is proud of you.
Most of all, I am proud of you.

Accomplishment is a small word to describe all
you have been through.
Your job is difficult for a man.
For a woman to be accepted and succeed is phenomenal.

I know it wasn't easy.
You studied hard, trained hard, and worked hard.
It was an uphill battle all the way.
There was a mountain to climb, and you climbed it.
There were bridges to burn, and you burned them.

Blood, sweat, and tears, and that's a fact—no cliché.

The dangers were many.
I worried all the time.
the hours must have seemed endless to you.
Struggle and sacrifice were a reality.

Through it all, you held your head high.
Railroading was in your blood.
Your lust to ride the rails was all you could see.
You looked beyond anything that got in your way.
You persevered, and you succeeded.

Your dedication to your job and fellow workers
was admirable.
All who know you respect you.

I know railroading will always be your first love.
Your heart beats a little faster every time
you climb on the engine.
You feel the power, you are in command, you pull the load.
Such great responsibility rests on your little shoulders.

I've seen the love in your eyes and the smile on your face
Every time you are around a train.
In spite of the toils, the rewards were many.
No one can ever say you didn't give it your all.

Every time I hear the whistle blow, I'll think of you.
If there is a forever, we'll ride the rails of gold to glory.
You'll be my engineer and lead me safely home.

I know you didn't quit.
You chose to move on
to ride the rails
in a different direction.

Walk tall, little sister.
Stand proud.
You are one hell of an amazing lady.

Locomotives Susie Operated

Susie's career as a professional railroad engineer in the mid/late twentieth century gave her the opportunity of operating many different class locomotives, some of them retired and in historical museums.

Pennsylvania Railroad

Pennsylvania Class GG1 4935

Pennsylvania Class GG1 4800 retired

Retired Locomotives Once Operated by Susie Housed in the Railroad Museum of Pennsylvania Strasburg, Pennsylvania

Class E44, electric, retired, Pennsylvania Railroad

Class E60, electric, retired, Pennsylvania Railroad

Class AEM7, electric, retired, Pennsylvania Railroad

EMD Class GP30, diesel, retired

Diesels Operated by Susie

EMD Class GP38, diesel
EMD Class GP40 and GP40-2, diesel
EMD Class SD40, diesel
EMD Class SD45, diesel
EMD GP7, GP9
EMD GP15-1
SW1200, SW1500
GE Dash8 series
GE UB series
GE UB, Class E8, diesel

In 1976, Susie may have been the first woman to sit behind the controls of a Class E8, *The Amtrak Empire*, out of Buffalo with an engineer and crew. She was twenty-three.

EMD Class SD40-2, diesel

EMD Class F40PH diesel

Acknowledgments

Thank you to Richard D. Spence, retired former president and CEO of ConRail, for believing in me and giving me the chance to make my railroad dream a reality.

Thanks to all the railroad crews out of the Frontier and Bison yards of Buffalo Division, New York, who encouraged me at the age of twenty-three to go after my dream to become an engineer.

Special thanks to my friend DJ, railroad engineer, Baltimore Division, with nineteen years with CSX for the encouragement to keep going when I became overwhelmed with writing this book.

Special thanks to Albert "Berky" Berkowitz and residents of Applewood Loomis Communities, Amherst, Massachusetts, who encouraged me to write this book.

I salute the heroic men and women, dedicated railroad workers risking their lives every day when they climb aboard their trains to get passengers safely to their destinations and tons of freight to businesses and homes across this great country of ours.

Susie Gaglia, 1979

About the Author

Growing up near active railroads, Susie Gaglia heard at an early age the captivating call of the lonesome whistle and sounds of trains through day and night. As she grew into adulthood, events in her life evolved so that she had direct contact with railroad operating personnel, and in time, she joined their ranks. Soon she became a qualified engineer and pulled countless freight and passenger trains during her fifteen-year railroad career.

When no longer a railroad employee, she continued drawn trackside by the call of a locomotive whistle, the sound of flanged wheels clattering over steel rails, or the pounding of a mighty locomotive working a grade.

A resident of Athol, Massachusetts, Susie works with night security at The Loomis Communities, Applewood at Amherst Retirement campus in Amherst, Massachusetts.

Railroads remain forever in Susie's blood. She has memories of her days in the righthand seat of a locomotive cab. Susie especially treasures having ridden the rails as part of America's rich railroad history.

Colophon

Text for *An American Railroad Dream* is set in Janson, the name given to a set of old-style serif typefaces from the Dutch Baroque period and modern revivals from the twentieth century. Janson is a crisp, relatively high-contrast serif design, most popular for body text.

Janson is based on surviving matrices from Leipzig named for Anton Janson (1620–1687), a Leipzig-based printer and punch-cutter from the Netherlands believed to have created them.

Titles are set in Kabel, a sans-serif typeface designed by German designer Rudolf Koch and released by the Klingspor foundry from 1927 onwards.

Kabel belongs to the geometric style of sans-serifs, popular in Germany at the time of Kabel's creation. Based loosely on the structure of the circle and straight lines, it nonetheless applies a number of unusual design decisions, such as a delicately low x-height, a quirky tilted *e*, and irregularly angled terminals, to add delicacy and an irregularity suggesting stylish calligraphy. A variety of rereleases and digitisations have been created.

CPSIA information can be obtained
at www.ICGtesting.com
Printed in the USA
BVHW021401230821
615019BV00002B/33